Published by Still Standing Publishing Company
Cover photo by Jaudon Photography
Glass of Raspberry Lemonade by Jaclyn Bell
Creative Direction: Shirley A. Merritt

Printed in the United States of America

ISBN-13: 978-0999336236
ISBN-10: 0999336231

DEDICATION

I dedicate this book to my beloved parents, James Rhea and Constance Allegra Merritt. Mommy, you were the perfect example of what a mother should be. Daddy, you were a wonderful role model for me. You are the reason I am such a strong, independent woman today. Also, I dedicate this story to my dearest brother Peter James. You were the epitome of unconditional love. Thank you for teaching me how to love completely. I felt the presence of each of you while writing my memoir. I hope you all are very pleased with my finished work and the way I told our story.

ACKNOWLEDGMENTS

I want to first give thanks to my Lord and Savior, Jesus Christ. Heavenly Father, you have truly blessed me with a gift... a love and passion for writing. Thank you for giving me the talent of turning the thoughts, words and memories in my head, into a story.

I want to thank Tamiko Lowry-Pugh for this opportunity. I appreciate your patience and guidance through this process.

I'm giving a heartfelt thank you to my sister Cynthia Merritt for taking time out of your busy schedule to read my memoir and write my Foreword.

I want to thank Cynthia Quarterman and Sandra Poole for assisting me with some of the proofreading and editing of my rough draft. Your knowledge and suggestions are key.

Thank you to my friend and photographer Carl Johnson. I applaud you and your work. I value your professionalism.

Last but certainly not least, thanks to my family and friends for your prayers and the support of my project. I hope you enjoy reading it as much as I did writing it.

CONTENTS

FOREWORD

I can recall reading an article in the daily newspaper in 1980; I was sitting on the floor at a sleepover with some girlfriends. We were all sitting in the den having conversation, laughing and just enjoying each other's company. I sat on the floor and read the article. It was the story of a young girl telling that her mother had basically been robbed of her life as she knew it, by the diagnosis of multiple sclerosis.

She told of her mother's busy life with her father, siblings, and herself. She was only 37 when diagnosed, and she was wheelchair bound at the time of the article. I was strongly affected as I read on and I couldn't believe that this disease came in and took away her normal life of functioning with a busy family life as well as her mobility away. I can recall calling everyone in the room to attention as I read the article aloud to them with urgency and shock.

I shouted it (as they say) "From the mountain top", telling so many people about this article over the next 35 years. This article affected me so strongly, and I never knew why until 1997, when I was diagnosed with MS. I then thought that was the reason I was so devastated by the article. However, MS is different for each individual affected by it, and it has not affected me in that same way. As I interact with Shirley and am now reading her memoir, it is apparent to me why I was so strongly affected by the article. The revelation was made to me, and now I see clearly that it was Shirley's story that I read about in 1980 and it gripped me and held on firmly for the next 37 years.

I am Shirley's younger sister, and we are not far apart in age. Throughout our lives, I can recall seeing the joy on Shirley's face whenever she was writing. The day she told me she was sharing her story in her memoir I was ecstatic. For as long as I can remember, writing has brought joy to Shirley's life and what a storyteller she is! Mommy was also a writer so you might say that it came to her honestly. Throughout her life, the topics of the stories she wrote would reflect the circumstances she was experiencing in life. The topics included; love, hurt, betrayal, joy, happiness, and pain, to name a few.

As I read through the pages of this memoir I felt the healing and strengthening this book offers to anyone who is: struggling with acceptance, fearful of a life-changing circumstance, and seeks to live a purposeful, selfless life that is enriched with the Grace and Mercy of God. She has blessed us with this book. As you read you will take away a great number of epiphanies and paradigm shifts that will assist in guiding you in coping with any type of life altering situation while walking in the journey of this life to reach a peaceful and purposeful destination.

She ended each chapter with an applicable scripture, and I would like to do the same...I think of this scripture when I play the video of her life in my mind.

"Be still and know that I am God." Psalm 46:10
Cynthia J. Merritt

INTRODUCTION

After living a typical and normal, seemingly healthy existence, imagine receiving a medical report that would change your life forever. Do you know quite how you would react to hearing such devastating news? What if the information were the unthinkable? Could you accept it, and would you be able to cope with the reality? It is my hope that after reading my story, you will learn how to develop your emotional strength, wisdom and good common sense, obedience, patience and most importantly, faith. You will acquire the knowledge of how to uncover positive attributes within yourself which happen to be necessary and are invaluable.

Practice these very powerful suggestions in order to develop courage: demonstrate undying faith in God or your higher power, pray without ceasing, eliminate words such as cannot, impossible, self-conscious, try, embarrassed, ashamed and defeated from your mindset, and replace them with favorable and enthusiastic words. Never let fear control your thoughts.

My reason for writing my memoir, is to share a very condensed version of my life story with you. Unfortunate circumstances are inevitable. However, we were created to be able to continue existing despite the unforeseen conditions. I hope my life story will serve as a medium to inspire, motivate and uplift those individuals who are experiencing a similar situation, especially those finding it difficult to cope. It is my goal to encourage you to adapt a new frame of mind. So, you too can make the very best of your life and turn your lemons into something great.

Each chapter encompasses factual stories about my life, and I've ended each one with a relevant scripture or quote. My memoir covers a period of 40 years pre-diagnosis and 16 years post. I have included many facts regarding multiple sclerosis throughout the story. Also, you will find information in the latter part of the book that may be resourceful to someone battling a debilitating situation.

Now, please join me on this journey of my life, beginning with chapter one.

CHAPTER 1
Jim and Connie

My name is Shirley Anne. My father chose the name Shirley. However, my mother wanted to name me Angelina. She gave in, and they compromised. My name most definitely describes who I am. It means that I am extremely spiritual. I am very motivating and inspiring, and I firmly encourage others to be the same way. I am instinctive, compassionate, grateful, loving and devoted, as well as exuberant, and I've been told that I add sunshine to everyone's day. I was born on September 6, 1961 in Altadena, California, to James Rhea and Constance Allegra Merritt, much better known as Jim and Connie. My father was from San Diego, California, and my mother was from Chicago, Illinois. It was a very significant year, one that went down in history.

In addition to my birth, the United States launched a capsule named Freedom 7 with Astronaut Alan B. Shepherd. I am the middle child. My older brother is Peter James, and 15 months later in 1962, I would have a little sister named Cynthia Josephine. The year of her birth had a very similar importance, for John Glen orbited the earth before going up into space. Cynthia looks like Mommy, and I am my daddy's twin. However, I do get my height from my mother. She was five-one, and I am five-one and a half.

My parents adopted Peter because after three miscarriages, they began to think my mother wasn't going to be able to carry a baby full term. They were very happy to have been blessed with Peter. They loved him so much. Daddy has told us stories about how he kept Peter under his wing (protected) because he was so accident-prone. He said if someone threw a football, Peter was sure to get hit in the head with it.

I was my mother's first full term pregnancy. So, my daddy called me "The Survivor." However, I didn't know about this nickname until he told me about it later on after I was an adult. My sister was her second full term pregnancy. I've heard that when you've miscarried, then had a successful pregnancy, there is no more pressure to have a baby, so the next pregnancy is much easier.

Altadena is about 14 miles from downtown Los Angeles and just north of Pasadena, the city known for the Rose Bowl.

We were my mother's pride and joy. She wouldn't and did not put anything before her children. Once she had babies, she decided to stop working and began her new occupation, "homemaker." I remember that she was always in the kitchen preparing meals or cleaning and doing things around the house to make a lovely home for her family. She loved decorating, and she put her heart and soul into it. You really could feel the love in every room. Our home was beautiful. I can actually remember almost everything about it. Due to Mommy's decorating skills, it probably could have been in House and Garden magazine.

She always showed us just how much she loved us. Aunt Bettye has told me that she once asked my mother, "Why do you make three different meals for your children"? She replied, "Because they are three different little people with three separate personalities, and they don't like the same things."

Cooking was one of her favorite things to do for us. I remember her baking homemade enchiladas, gingerbread and monkey bread. I even remember her making liver and onions, boiled chicken wings or turkey tails and rice... oh and chitterlings for Daddy. Cynthia, Peter and I would not eat them though because we didn't like the smell. There were a lot of things I didn't like to eat. Mommy said I was a finicky eater. I remember she would have to make things special for me. Otherwise, I just wouldn't eat. I wouldn't eat mayonnaise because I didn't like it. My sister and I wanted butter instead on our sandwiches. I wouldn't eat the crust, so she always had to trim the edges first. I remember that Cynthia's favorite was a peanut butter and butter sandwich, and my favorite was cheese and bread with nothing on it. I think Peter liked jelly with his peanut butter and lunch meat (also known as cold cuts) with his cheese. She could leave the crust on the bread for him and Cynthia.

My parents actually took me to the doctor once because I stopped eating. He told them not to worry because I would eat when I was hungry enough, and I would eventually outgrow this behavior. That I did because eating is definitely one of my favorite things to do now. I remember one instance when I wouldn't eat my dinner. Mommy said I couldn't get up from the table until I finished. Well, I knew the garbage disposal was under the sink because of the loud noise. I also knew that it made food disappear, especially food that you did not want to eat. So, when everyone left me alone in the kitchen at the table, I opened the cabinet doors and scraped the food off of my plate, to underneath the sink. I thought I was rid of it. I thought it was gone, and so did Mommy... that is until she found it. I got the spanking of my life, to say the least... back then it was with a belt. As tiny and skinny as I was, let's just say I felt every bit of it!

One thing I hated was beets, and I still do to this day. I wouldn't eat them then, and I won't eat them now. Anyway, I wanted her to be proud of me. So, I actually found the courage somehow, to eat the ones she put on my plate one day. I could hardly wait to brag on myself because I knew that when I told her, she would smother me with hugs and kisses and tell me how proud she was of me. I loved to get attention, and she was really good at making us feel special. She always found ways to show us that we meant the world to her.

Mommy was so very domestic. She even made our Barbie doll clothes herself on the sewing machine. She made sure that Cynthia and I had all of the accessories that came with Barbie. We each had our own green Barbie convertible. However, we didn't have the doll house. She would let us use the linen cabinet, make believing it was their apartments.

We did have a playroom though. It used to be Grandpa Merritt's room before he passed away. He lived with us in his old age until he died at 97. He suffered from dementia. My daddy always said I looked just like Grandpa. He said I even walked like him. Like me, Grandpa had slew feet. Daddy used to say to me, "You know that funny duck-like walk you have? Well, you get it from your grandpa." I've never seen a picture of him as a young man, but I can tell that he was very handsome. Grandpa's father was a Portuguese sailor, and his mother was Black. Daddy said Grandpa, whose name was Matthew Merritt, had two families. He said he just up and walked away from one and started another one with the help... who was my father's mother, Essie. He said he was a distant father and didn't have much involvement with any of his children's lives, especially after they were grown up. When he was old and became ill, my mother wanted him to live with us. We would take care of him because none of my father's siblings would even consider doing it. His dementia was really bad. He would see and hear things quite frequently. Daddy's mother Essie, died in her early 50s because of a stomach virus. So, we never knew her.

My mother loved doing special things for us like having birthday parties, and holidays meant so much to her. I only remember one birthday party, and I don't really remember very much about it, except that I had on a pretty new pink, orange and yellow dress with a big pointed white collar. We had the party on the back patio with my family and friends. I remember a birthday cake on a table in the middle of the patio, and that's all.

Christmas was the best time for our little family. On Christmas Eve, we would all watch Christmas cartoons and specials on the television set while eating Christmas treats. Once they sent us to bed, they would set our toys up under the tree and all over the family room. When we woke up early in the morning, we would be so surprised and excited. We would play all day long while Mommy stayed in the kitchen preparing the holiday meal. Daddy loved to eat pecans and walnuts while watching TV in the family room. Mommy kept a basket of them with one of those silver metal nutcrackers on the coffee table. So, he was usually doing that or playing his horn in their room at the other end of the house. Daddy played the saxophone.

I loved the Christmas season because our mommy decorated the entire house. She put artificial snowflakes on the table tops with figurines of Santa's sleigh, Rain deer, Frosty the snowman, Christmas trees and of course, the Nativity scene with baby Jesus. I could hardly wait for her homemade Butterball cookies with pecans and powdered sugar to be ready (a recipe that my sister has now perfected). Oh, how I loved Christmas at our house. We always had a real tree with tinsel, a shining star, different colored bulbs, lights and lots of presents.

My mother had a couple of other passions, they were writing and playing the piano. She wrote articles and poetry on subjects such as Negro history. She even submitted some of her manuscripts to Ebony magazine and intended to publish a book of poetry in her future. Also, she self-published two spiritual hymns in 1968. They were entitled, "This Is It" and "Contented."

Years ago, Daddy and I flew out to San Diego to visit his sister, Aunt Laverne... and Uncle Clinton. My aunt was dying of cancer. One day she called me over to her piano bench and said, "I have a surprise for you." She opened up the top of the bench, reached inside and pulled out two pieces of paper. It was the sheet music for my mother's two songs. I feel that my love for writing came from my mother.

Of course, we took piano lessons. Mrs. Blackwell was our piano teacher. She was a taller, shapely lady with very fair skin. It was clearly, a characteristic of her Caucasian ancestry. Next to Mommy, she was the prettiest lady I had ever seen. I remember her wearing red or orange lipstick and lots of black eyeliner. Her hair was long and black. It was a beautiful mixture of straight and curly locks. She always wore fitted pencil skirts, and she wore high heeled pumps like Mommy.

Mommy took care of the inside, and Daddy took care of the outside of our house. He planted ivy, moss, flowers and trees. His brother Uncle Matthew (Padno was his nickname), laid the cement patio and built a low concrete wall in the backyard to keep us from falling over the edge and down the hill. You see, we lived up in the California hills, and the valley was down below. On a clear night, you could actually see the Rose Bowl from our back yard. Daddy loved working in the yard back then, and our yard was one of the nicest in the neighborhood. He was so very proud of it.

My daddy was a mailman. My brother, sister and I got such a kick out of this. We felt like our daddy had such a neat job. Back in those days, they wore the mailman uniform, hat and all. They even walked from house to house, and they carried the brown leather mail bag on their shoulder. Everyone even had a milkman, and he actually left bottles of milk on the front porches.

I had such an imagination. I had a crush on "Jethro the ice cream man." I gave him that name because he looked like "Jethro Bodine" from my favorite hit TV series, "The Beverly Hillbillies." The funny thing is that I can actually still remember the music that came from his truck, letting us know to run and get money for ice cream. I was so unaware of the racial conflict and division that existed. Things seemed different back then. You didn't hear about car jackings and doors being kicked in on the news, but there was another type of violence. My world seemed calm and safe. We attended Pasadena Christian School because it was private, and during that time, I remember it being predominately White. Undeniably, I know that racial discrimination existed in the 60s, but I guess my parents sheltered us from the realities of it. I was incognizant about the logic of why little Black girls shouldn't develop crushes on little White boys... because I did. I often think about that time of innocence.

I sure wish I could remember, but Daddy would say when I was little, I used to take off running like a Jack-rabbit. He said he would have to chase me to catch me because I ran so fast. I had knock-knees, slightly bowed legs and slew-feet. It seems like I would have tripped up over my own two feet with all of that going on. I did fall quite a bit, but I guess my parents didn't worry about it at all because this was typical of any young child. It was as if I lacked coordination. I just tried to act like a big girl. I would pick myself up and hold back the tears. Then I would try to keep from blushing when my parents and other grown-ups would say, "Oh, she didn't even cry."

The same thing happened when I tried to hula hoop, jump rope, hopscotch or even play the games paddle ball and jacks. I just didn't have the coordination. So, even though I really wanted to play these games, I didn't because I wasn't any good at them. I was amazed at and wondered how other kids were, with so little effort. My brother Peter was always very good at playing most hand games, especially marbles. So, my sister Cynthia and I just played with our Barbie dolls and paper dolls most of the time. Besides, we always had so much fun. Also, we went over to our friend's houses next door and up the street and played... dolls usually. Daddy taught us all how to ride bicycles. I liked this because I didn't seem to have any problems with riding my bike.

In the evenings, our family took walks around the block. Mommy and Daddy had several good friends on our street, and we were friends with their kids as well. Most of our neighbors were Caucasian. We would pass the Pixley's who lived next door, Omar and Judy, an inter-racial couple a few houses away and the Sloan's lived up the street on the corner. Peter's best friend Jacque who was

Black, lived around the curve and down the street. I never saw him, but our parents said Ivan Dixon, the Black actor from the television series "Hogan's Heroes," also lived in the same neighborhood.

Sometimes, our parents would take us for evening drives. We had a brand new yellow Chevrolet Impala station wagon. First, we would take our baths and then put on our pajamas. Our parents would load us up with blankets and pillows, into the back seat of the station wagon. We called it the "Waaay back seat." Sometimes, we went to a drive-in movie, and sometimes Daddy would just take us on a scenic drive around Pasadena and the Los Angeles County area. It really didn't matter to us where we went. We just loved riding around in the back of that station wagon, and the longer the drive, the better. We could look out of the rear window and see the moon and the stars trailing behind, as Daddy drove us through the city. When they took us to the drive-in, we usually ended up falling asleep before the movie ended, but it was still so much fun anyway.

It was really a treat if they took us through the drive-thru at one of our favorite restaurants. We loved to eat burgers and fries at Jack in the Box. My favorite food was chili dogs and orange pop from Der Wienerschnitzel.

Sometimes, it was a trip down Sunset Strip, (a part of Sunset Boulevard). It's a mile-and-a-half long and goes through West Hollywood. When Daddy was in the mood to drive fast, he would take us onto the Los Angeles freeway. No matter which excursion they chose to take us on for the evening, we would be asleep by the time we made it back home to Loma Alta Drive, but then they already knew this. Hence, the reason for the blankets and pillows.

Mommy was a disciplinarian, and we certainly had our share of rules to follow. We had a daily schedule. We had lunch time, nap time, snack time, play time, homework and study time, time to color, time to take piano lessons, time for watching television and probably some more times that I'm forgetting to mention.

We were not allowed to be in the living room without an adult. The only times I remember us being in there was when Mommy was

22

playing her piano, or Daddy was playing his saxophone. His favorite jazz sax player and musical influence was Mr. Lester Young. Stan Getz was another favorite, and he loved playing his hit "Girl from Ipanema" for us. It is one of my favorites even today, and when Daddy played his horn, he sounded just like him.

We were not allowed to answer the telephone, especially if Mommy was not at home. We were not allowed to get up from a nap until she told us we could. I'll never forget the time we decided that we were going to play a trick on her. We were supposed to be asleep because it was nap time. For some reason, we thought that we would get up early. We actually stuffed pillows under the covers and snuck out of the room. Of course, she came in and immediately knew that the lumps in the twin beds were not her children. Needless to say, when she finally caught up with us, we knew we had made the biggest mistake of our young lives. In those times, when Cynthia and I were the lone culprits and Mommy was too tired to run after us, she would send big brother Peter after us, and he would bring us to her for our disciplinary action.

We weren't allowed to leave the table unless we finished our plate. I mentioned that earlier. We were surely not allowed to ride our bikes without either her or Daddy knowing. We didn't realize it then, but that was for our own good. It was so that we wouldn't fall off and scrape up our knees and elbows. Mommy didn't want us to have scars on our legs.

We were not allowed to go into the refrigerator without asking. Besides, we really didn't need to because she always surprised us with our favorites at snack time. I can remember her bringing little saucers of treats in to us while we were playing. She always gave us snacks like cold cuts, raisins, fruit or cheese and graham crackers. Sometimes, she would surprise us with fig cookies or those chewy orange slices with the sugar on the outside.

I loved it when Mommy and Daddy let us take our baths in their bathroom. They had a 1960s garden tub with a glass wall. You could look out into a small flower garden surrounded by a tall redwood fence no wider than the length of the bathtub. It was so pretty. This was just another very creative and special thing she came up with to make our home beautiful.

I did not understand it nor was I ever able to figure out why, but occasionally I used to have nightmares, and sometimes they were about Mommy. One night I dreamed she was dancing in the flames of our fireplace naked. I didn't know what it meant, and I never told her about the dream. Another time I dreamed she left to go to the store, but before she left, she told us not to answer the phone. Well, as soon as she pulled out of the garage and driveway I was tested because the phone rang, and I did the very thing that I was not supposed to do. I answered it. As I held the receiver to my face and said, "hello," I saw her head turn completely around backward, while she was driving away in the car and down the street. Her eyes were big and completely bucked. She was staring right at me. Now, how could she see me through the window and the curtains while she was driving away from our house, and how could I see her? Well, because this was a dream. In fact, it was a nightmare! Then one time I dreamed she died. I woke up crying, and she came down the hall to our bedroom. She asked me what was the matter? I said, "I dreamed you died." I'll never forget what she said because it hurt my feelings. She said, "Well I didn't, so go back to sleep."

To everyone else, Jim and Connie Merritt seemed like the perfect couple with the perfect family, living in the perfect house of their dreams, but everything wasn't as perfect as it seemed. Sometimes, at night when we were supposed to be asleep, we would hear them arguing. It seemed like they would scream abusive words to each other at the top of their lungs. If we managed to be sleeping through it, at some point, I would almost always be awakened by Mommy telling me to get up and come and go with her because we were leaving. We would go down the hallway where she would tell me to wait, and she would go back into their bedroom and start fussing at Daddy again.

To be honest, my daddy wasn't an argumentative kind of person unless he was provoked. On the other hand, according to Daddy, my mother came from a family who liked sarcasm and quarreling. After we were grown up of course, he would tell us stories about how her family would constantly bicker and insult each other. He would say, "And their own mother would encourage them by finding some humor in it." He told us, she would sit there listening and just laugh because she thought it was funny. Anyway, after standing in the hallway for a while, I would just start crying because I was so sleepy and just wanted to go back to my room. Eventually, they would stop squabbling, and she would tell me to go get back in my bed.

My mommy was overweight. I don't know what her weight was, but it was too much for her small frame. She was only five-one. When she and Daddy first married, she was tiny. She gained the weight as a result of her pregnancies. She developed high blood pressure and was on medication for her condition.

One Sunday morning in 1968 Mommy made breakfast for us. Daddy was in the family room. We went to our rooms to get ready for church, and Mommy went down the hall to their bedroom. Suddenly, we heard Mommy yell out Daddy's name, "Jim"! Daddy ran to her and we followed. She told him that she felt like she was on fire. He told her to stand in the shower under cool running water while he called an ambulance. She did not make it to their bathroom before passing out on the floor. I remember her eyes were wide open, big and completely bucked. She defecated and Daddy told Peter to go and get tissue paper. I saw her bottom. It was taking the ambulance too long to come, so Daddy had another emergency vehicle transport her to the hospital, and he went with them. When Daddy finally came home, he told us that our mommy had passed away. He said she wouldn't be coming back home, and our entire world changed that day.

She had a cerebral hemorrhage-a stroke, and though it was 49 years ago, I remember it as though it was yesterday. I have always believed those nightmares that I used to have about Mommy were premonitions because in one dream, she was in the fire naked. In another, her eyes were bucked, and in one, she actually died. We were going to have to get used to living in our house without our mommy. I remember feeling like I didn't know how I was going to do this.

When Daddy took us to view her body at the funeral home, he told us that we could touch her. I touched her cheek, and it was cold and hard. Our daddy was very nurturing, as he explained what was happening to Mommy's body and why she felt so unusual. I don't remember much about the funeral. Although, I think her dress was a pastel blue with ruffles around the collar.

The following days felt really different around our house, and I remember feeling sad and lonely. I was depressed. There was a mop on the patio. I would pull a string out every day to sort of represent each day that she was gone. I don't remember for how long I did this, probably until the mop was moved. My sister and I found it hard to have fun as we played with our paper and Barbie dolls. We missed our mommy's presence so much. We used to look forward to her telling us that it was lunch time and just looking in on us.

I know Peter missed her also. When he was little, he would sometimes hold on to the end of her dress, as if that was his own little way of making sure that she didn't leave him. I probably wasn't even born yet, but I've seen the photos. I'm so thankful that Mommy liked to take plenty of pictures because I have the photos to remind me of her, but then how could I ever forget?

Everyone was so kind and wanted to help Daddy with us. All of a sudden, he was a single parent with three little kids. He and our mommy had a lot of close friends. Mrs. Ray would come by every morning and bring our school lunches. I guess she didn't know how finicky I was because she would make sandwiches that I was just not going to eat. She made hamburgers with mayonnaise, mustard and pickle relish. Sometimes, she made tuna fish and egg salad. Mommy never made those things. So, I would eat the potato chips and snack cakes, but that was all.

Daddy just had surgery on his right arm before Mommy died. He still had stitches, and he wore a sling. You should have seen him trying to brush our long, thick hair with one good arm and the hand only, of the other arm which was in the sling. I guess he soon realized that he needed some help because Uncle Matthew, Aunt Bettye and their baby, my first cousin, moved into our house to help him take care of us. They lived with us for about a year. Anyway, Aunt Bettye was a big help with us. She did the cooking, and she did our hair too. That must have been a huge relief for Daddy. Aunt Bettye taught me and Cynthia so much, and she quickly became my favorite aunt. Aunt Bettye was so pretty, and I just loved it when people would say I looked just like her, even though I really looked just like my daddy's clone. Having Aunt Bettye in the house made everything so much better. She took my mind off of missing my mommy so much and made it feel like home again. I know she was a God-send to our daddy, but she was also just what Cynthia and I needed because we were little girls.

And This Too Shall Pass
Unknown

Our father and our piano teacher Mrs. Blackwell, who was now estranged from her spouse, were becoming good friends. So, when she told him that she decided to move herself and her three children back to her hometown of Huntsville, Alabama... Daddy made the decision to move his family as well and see what the South had to offer him. That's right, talk about making a spontaneous decision. Shortly afterward, one evening we climbed into Daddy's bed to watch television, as we often did. That's when he decided to tell us that we were moving. He said, "Well, you guys... we're moving to the South where the people talk funny." We just snickered and giggled while he imitated the Southerners by speaking slang. Daddy didn't waste any time selling our house either.

"Do not grieve, for the joy of the Lord is your strength."
Nehemiah 8:10

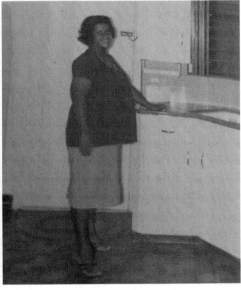

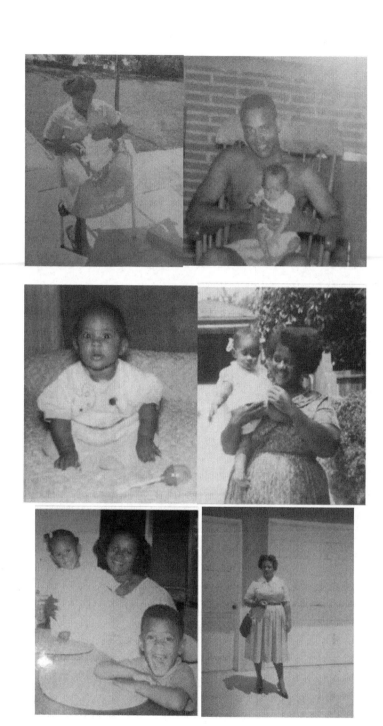

CHAPTER 2
The Move to Alabama

I don't remember all of the daily and hourly details of our move from Altadena, California to Huntsville, Alabama. However, I do know that once we were there, it seemed like an entirely different world to us. I could see that living in the South was going to be a whole new way of life, and I really didn't know if I was going to like it. My siblings and I were about to get our very first lessons in racial discrimination.

Huntsville, Alabama is a city that is well-known for the Redstone Arsenal and the Space and Rocket Center. It is nicknamed "The Rocket City" because of the association it has with the U.S. space missions. What a coincidence it was that we were moving to a city which had profound connections relating to the years that we were born. Huntsville also has many chemical and manufacturing plants.

When we first arrived, we stayed with Mrs. Blackwell's aunt Helen. She lived in an old Antebellum mansion on Daisy Avenue. It reminded me of a haunted house because it needed repairs and paint. It appeared that no one was caring for the yard which was surrounded by a barbed wire fence. I'll never forget it because thanks to Peter, I have a scar on my face to always remind me. He was giving me a ride on his bike one evening and ran directly into the fence. He said he couldn't see it because the sun was going down. It barely missed my eye. I actually spent the next few decades resenting Mrs. Blackwell for not applying cocoa butter to it so it would disappear. Mommy definitely would have thought of that. The scar was ugly, and it made me cry. I'm sure glad that back then I didn't know, I would have it for the rest of my life. I probably would have been devastated.

Anyway, all of the houses on this street were in this same exact condition. I was only eight years old, but I was aware enough to wonder why Daddy wanted to leave our nice home in California and come here and live in this ugly one. Everything in this house was old and kind of depressing to me, and the wooden floors creaked when you walked on them. That was so creepy. All four of us had to share one room, and the bathroom was out of date, dark and drafty. I don't remember how long we stayed in her house, but I know Daddy definitely enrolled us into Terry Heights Elementary school immediately, while we were still living there.

Mrs. Blackwell would come and pick us up in the mornings for school. She would take us, including her oldest daughter. Her two little ones had not started yet. She would bring scrambled egg sandwiches with white bread or "Light bread," as they called it, but the crust was still on it. However, I do remember eating the sandwich anyway and actually, kind of liking it. Until this day, I like scrambled egg sandwiches... but I like wheat bread, toasted and with butter.

Finally, we moved into our own house. It was on Hammonds Drive. It was a gold brick house with a car-port, steps and a short sidewalk which led to the house. I approved of this one. It was nice. Mrs. Blackwell and her children used to come over. When I was 10, she taught me how to cook my first dish. It was macaroni and cheese. Sometimes, she did things for us like wash our hair. We found ourselves getting very used to her being in our lives. We even started calling her Mommy. So, you can probably only imagine how we felt when she and Daddy suddenly stopped being friends. She went to Mr. Blackwell. Daddy said she felt sorry for him because he had been beaten up just for being a Black man in some other small town in the South.

It was sad. I remember feeling like we lost another mother. I don't think much about it now of course, but back then I did wonder how Daddy must have felt. It must have been hard on him, especially since he had just moved us that far away from our home. I couldn't help but think about that. I felt empathy for him, even though I was just a child.

Daddy always rented the houses we lived in. In fact, he never bought another house again. I guess that is the main reason why we moved so often, and each house never really felt like it was home.

Children are really very resilient because after we left California, although I know I still loved her and would never forget her, I didn't think about and miss Mommy as much anymore. At our very young ages, we were latchkey kids. We would come home from school to an empty house because our father was at work selling real estate. That was his new profession. We were left at home most of the time with no parental supervision. I remember getting fussed at or even a whipping when Daddy came home sometimes because we had broken something, and he did use his belt. Cynthia and I would tattletale on Peter so he would be the only one to get in trouble, just to keep ourselves from feeling Daddy's wrath and getting punished.

Our family life just wasn't the same anymore. Daddy wasn't at home much, even when he wasn't working. He did always leave the phone numbers to his whereabouts by the phone, so we could reach him if we needed him. Honestly, we did use them quite often, and it seemed like we called him every evening when we were hungry for dinner. In fact, we had to call him two or three times. You see, our father had taken up shooting pool, and one of his friends was Mr. Jamie Toney, a professional. He was one of the best pool players around. He also frequently played the fiddle with a country and western band on television. He had a family oriented billiard room, and our daddy practically lived there when he wasn't working. He would even take us there every once in a while, on the weekends. Daddy would finally leave there, bring us dinner and go back out to the pool room. Dinner was usually fast food like tacos, burgers and fries or pizza.

A couple of nights a week Daddy would cook a good meal, and he would have dinner with us. He only knew how to cook two things... broiled chicken or broiled hamburgers, and the side dishes were canned. He would make canned Spanish rice, mixed vegetables, turnip greens, pinto beans, his favorite-hominy, which I hated and just wouldn't eat. Then last but not least, canned macaroni and cheese. That's right, there was a popular brand name that made a canned macaroni and cheese, but don't knock it because it really wasn't that bad at all. I almost forgot, sometimes he made us canned spaghetti and meatballs with grated Parmesan cheese on top, of course. He delegated responsibilities to each of us, so we all helped out with preparing dinner. One of us set the table. Somebody made the buttered toast, and someone made a pitcher of the flavored powdered drink mix. It's funny, but every once in a while, I get a craving for Daddy's broiled chicken. If I give in to it and cook it, as soon as I take one bite... I smile because I remember.

Needless to say, our diet consisted mainly of processed and canned foods. I don't blame or fault my father in any way though because he did the best that he could. He was just trying to feed us a well-balanced meal. He wanted to ensure that his kids didn't go hungry, and he really didn't know very much about nutrition and cooking. He was trying his best to play the roles of both parents. Besides, the small Black-owned real estate company that Daddy worked for wasn't paying him very much.

When Daddy spent time at home, my siblings and I would smile and whisper to each other, "We're having a fun family now." When he stayed home in the evenings, he usually just slept, played his horn or listened to his Johnny Mathis, Ray Charles or Ray Price albums. Ray was one of his favorites (both of them), and he liked listening to his most loved country music. Sometimes, when he was home, he would be back in his room putting a new relaxer in his hair. Daddy was wearing his hair like Al Sharpton, even though back then, I had not yet heard of Al Sharpton. Daddy adopted that look though because he wore his hair like that for the rest of his life.

It's funny, but I had become quite the domestic one in our household, since we no longer had a mother at home. I was only 10 years old, calling Daddy at his real estate office, asking him if he would bring a certain citrus scented furniture polish home so I could polish the furniture or a popular floor wax so I could make our kitchen floor shine. I would see these products on the TV commercials that came on in between the game shows and soap operas. The inside of our house looked nothing like our home did when Mommy was alive, even though we had the same furniture. It wasn't as clean and pretty, but I wanted to try and re-create the homely environment, if at all possible. Cynthia and I would bring our Easy Bake Oven into the kitchen and bake little cakes made out of pancake mix because Daddy didn't buy us the real cake, cookie and brownie mixes that were used with the oven, until Christmas.

We had very creative young minds. We played with our paper dolls every chance we could get and practically all-day long. We would draw them, and before we would cut them out, we'd trace their faces so that we could draw them in different outfits. This was how we would make believe they changed clothes. We used this same method when they went shopping for new clothes. We drew furniture for each house, and we had many different families and households. We literally had their neighborhoods set up all over our beds, dresser and the floor. We had such immense imaginations. We made an entire small city. To aggravate us, Peter would fling open the door with great force and blow the city of paper dolls all over the room! Cynthia and I would be furious, but we just simply gathered all of the paper people, clothes and furniture up and spread them all back out again. This would keep us in the room playing for hours.

There was one evening when Daddy wasn't at home with us. I guess we were trying to broil hamburgers in the oven, and it caught on fire. Peter ran through the backyard to his friend's house. He was a White boy named Terry. Terry's dad came back with him, and he brought a portable fire extinguisher. He sprayed the oven and put the fire out for us, but he didn't say much about it to us afterward. I remember him just turning and walking out. It was almost like he was just shaking his head in disbelief. He went back home through the backyard. Now, that was in the 70s, but if that happened today, Daddy probably would have been reported to the Division of Family and Children Services, and we might have been taken away from him.

When we were young, still in elementary school, my sister and I were little actresses. When school was out for summer break we watched soap operas every day, so we decided that we could create our own. All of the characters were played by just the two of us. We gave each one of them first and last names, just like on real TV shows. I don't know when we developed this talent, but it was surely inside of us, and one episode might go on for hours just like almost everything else she and I played together. It was during this time of my life that my new interest in acting began to unfold, and that interest would expand into my adulthood.

A profound memory that I have of my childhood is when I was introduced to what I will just refer to as, "My Black experience." Sometimes, Daddy would take us to one of his friend's house and let us spend the day with her kids. She and Daddy played religious music together. She played the piano. Daddy had a segment during the gospel hours on Sunday at a local Black radio station.

Her kids were really in touch with their modern day Black culture and individual Blackness. She had teenagers and one young child at home. When we went into their rooms, their walls were covered with posters of The Jackson Five, James Brown and all of the Motown artists from the R&B magazines. This was so different from who was on our walls. Our few posters were of the top pop artists from Tiger Beat magazine. They were pictures of David Cassidy and such.

Being introduced to the soul artists of the 70s was exciting, and I appreciated my Black education from our friends. I remember us kids marching around in their front yard chanting, "Say it loud-I'm Black and I'm proud" because her kids would tell us that we didn't act Black enough, and we didn't have soul.

Holidays were so very different from the ones we celebrated when our mother was alive. I don't remember Thanksgiving and Christmas dinners at all during the early 70s. So, that probably means that Daddy did not do anything special for us on those days.

When we were children, Daddy would pick up a Sears Christmas catalog in the fall and bring it home to us. He did this so that each of us could pick out toys that totaled 25 dollars or so. Every single day I would write down the page and item numbers of the toys I wanted. I carefully added them up, making sure not to go over the dollar amount, he gave us. The ironic thing was that on Christmas Eve, he would take us to JC Penney's toy department before they closed at about 6:00 PM, to see if they had the same toys that we found in the Sears catalog and buy them for us. He never bought another Christmas tree. So, he would tell us that we could just decorate the artificial Weeping Willow tree which was already a piece of décor in our living room. This tree was one of Mommy's creative decorating ideas. He left some of her pieces of furniture in storage, but for some reason, he brought this tree home. So, he would buy some balls, tinsel, garland, wrapping paper and tape at the store. When we came home, my siblings and I would decorate the tree, and Daddy would head back out to the pool room. We already knew what we had for Christmas presents, but we wanted to recreate some of those holiday memories from when Mommy was alive. So, we would wrap the unopened boxes of toys, put them under the decorated Weeping Willow tree and go to bed early because in the morning, we were going to get up, act like we were very surprised and joyfully open our presents.

Not particularly on Christmas Eve but we seriously wondered about this and asked each other... if we thought this man did something with our daddy and kidnapped us because he just didn't act the same anymore. To be honest, I sometimes thought that our daddy as we used to know him, checked out when Mommy died.

One summer, Daddy's older brother Uncle Ben and his wife Aunt Noonie, asked if we wanted to visit and spend our break with them in San Francisco, California. We did, so Daddy said we could, and he sent all three of us on a plane.

It felt good to be back in California, even though we had never been to San Francisco before. They had a son, a beautiful tan German Shepherd named Baron and her parents who lived across the street. They both worked in travel, one for the airport and one for the railroad. They had a nice home in the bay area. In the part of the city where they lived, the houses had no yards, and the streets were like asphalt hills with sidewalks. The houses were like stucco buildings with gates at the front doors, and they all had more than one story. Theirs had a steep flight of steps leading up to the front door. These houses were sure different from any others we had seen before. We really enjoyed it there.

Being around Aunt Noonie was good for me and Cynthia. She is the reason that I am such a girly-girl, now. She would fix our hair in the cutest little girl styles, with curly ponytails and kiss curls dangling in front of our ears. I remember my aunt touching up our edges with the straightening comb at the stove in the kitchen so that there would not be one hair out of place.

She looked forward to taking us shopping for new clothes. She told us that she just loved having little girls around. In fact, we went shopping every weekend. She would hide all of the bags in the trunk of the car, from Uncle Ben. Aunt Noonie drove a brown Ford Pinto, and it didn't have a trunk. So, she would borrow Uncle Ben's car whenever she planned a shopping pleasure trip. She loved to shop more than almost anything else. As a matter of fact, she recently told me that because she used to shop so much, she has enough clothes in her closet to last her another lifetime.

What I remember the most about Aunt Noonie is that she was a fashion trendsetter. Aunt Noonie always wore matching sandals, and she was a real Fashionista. Everything in her closet was extremely colorful and flowing like silk, rayon and chiffon. Each outfit had accessories to match, and she wore exquisite hairpieces which matched the silky texture of her own beautiful black hair as she has Native American ancestry.

She would dress me and Cynthia almost like twins. Sometimes, our outfits were exactly the same, and sometimes they were a different color or a bit of a different style. We were so cute and stylish in our hot pants and laced up Go-go boots. My boots were black, and Cynthia's were white. I just loved my bell bottoms and psychedelic blouses.

I wish they had taken more pictures of us that summer because I don't have many. There's one more thing that I want to mention about Aunt Noonie. She made the best Tamale Pie. It was like a big enchilada cooked in a skillet but with corn.

We made friends with the little Puerto Rican girl across the street. I remember walking up and down those hilly sidewalks and going to the corner deli to buy some of the ham and cheese sub sandwiches with pickles and mustard which were so good. I recall playing, or in my case, I was (trying to play) because of my lack of coordination, a rubber band jump rope game called high-jumps on the sidewalk. Now, it required a lot of skill. Good eye, leg, and foot coordination was imperative in order to be good at high-jumps. It was Chinese jump rope, an elastic skipping game. I was clumsy and awkward. So, I knew I had to settle for being mediocre. We had a lot of fun that summer.

Actually, I remember something else about that summer. My cousin had been listening to a new album. On the cover was an afro and maggots, *Maggot Brain*. It was the first time I had ever heard of the Black American funk band, Parliament- Funkadelic. They had a newly released album in July 1971. I guess I had finally developed an ear for funkier music, thanks to our afro-centric friends back in Huntsville, Alabama.

Summer was now over, yet we were still in California. I really didn't know why, but Daddy actually let us begin the school year there. We attended for a while. I don't really know how long. I don't think it was even a full semester when before I knew it, we were back in Alabama with Daddy.

We were gone for several months and had become so used to a family life with two adults at home. Now we had to get used to being at home by ourselves all over again, but this time things were a little different because every time we felt like Daddy wasn't acting the way our daddy should, we would call Aunt Noonie and Uncle Ben in

San Francisco and tell on him. We would show him, we thought to ourselves.

As soon as we arrived home from the airport and went to our bedrooms our eyes opened wide, and our jaws dropped. We couldn't believe what we were seeing. Our room was so pretty. We had pink laced curtains with white bedspreads. There were pink pillows on our twin beds, and there was a pink fluffy shag rug on the floor in between the two beds. We let out high pitched squeals. Peter's room was nice also. Although, I can't really remember what it looked like. I was so intrigued with ours that I guess I didn't pay his that much attention. I know it was a huge improvement though because previously, we referred to his room as "The dungeon."

Daddy made his way back to our rooms, and he was smiling. He was glad to see how happy this made us. He told us that he met a new female friend, and they had been seeing each other for a while now. (No wonder he left us in San Francisco so long.) He said she wanted to surprise us by decorating our rooms before we came home, and we would meet her soon. He also told us that she had a son, just under Cynthia's age. So, we did eventually meet Daddy's new friend and her son. We called her Ms. Baxter. She was married once before, and Baxter was actually her married name. However, she still used it.

She was a tall, dark brown skinned lady with a shapely figure. She had large breasts like Mommy and a pretty face. She had a beautiful home, and it was decorated so lovely. Often, she would cook and invite us over for dinner. She loved to cook, and we enjoyed eating her home cooked Southern meals. Besides, getting a break from eating processed, canned and fast food every night was a welcomed change.

She washed and pressed our hair on a regular basis. She styled it into two curled ponytails with a part down the middle. Sometimes, she gave us a bang, and every so often, she let it hang loose and long with curls that fell around my shoulders. I remember the first time I wore my hair down to school, the Black boys teased me and said that I had on a wig. It didn't bother me though. They were just not used to seeing long, soft-textured hair on a Black girl.

Like Mommy, she also enjoyed the holidays with all of the decorating, shopping for gifts and cooking. However, they were very different in every other way. They stayed together for several years. It was important to me that she made my daddy happy, and she did... at least for the time being.

So, we were moving into another house in a different kind of neighborhood. The real estate company that Daddy worked for owned houses in an underprivileged community. They made Daddy an offer. If he agreed to show the house, the rent would be free. In other words, the house was going to be a model home. Needless to say, he took the offer but remember, this was the 70s. You definitely could not do this today. The world that we live in now is much too dangerous. People who were house hunting, with or without agents, would come by and preview our house. It was newly remodeled, so honestly, it was one of the nicer houses, if not the nicest in the community.

Daddy began to impose some very strict rules. Of course, we felt like he was being too hard on us, but we were looking at it from a kid's perspective. As an adult, I know he must have felt that it was necessary in order to protect us from others, as well as from ourselves. After all, we were now becoming teenagers. Kids weren't allowed in the house. This was probably his toughest rule and the hardest one for us to follow because I remember sneaking our friends out of the front door when he would pull into the carport on the side of the house. Once, Peter got into some mischief for just being with some boys who were up to no good, and Daddy had to go and pick him up from some law authority office. I don't know what Peter was thinking because he was in so much trouble when Daddy brought him home, and that's all I will say about it.

It was in 1972, while we were living here in this house, that Daddy made the very hasty decision to move back to California. Although, I'm sure he was torn, this must have been something that he felt he needed to do. I don't know if he gave any consideration to how it might impact us. However, I was completely devastated. We were given no time to even try to process this news. We were told to pack our clothes only, leave everything else, and be ready to leave in a certain amount of time.

I literally became physically sick. You see, when I was a child, and actually all through high school, I was very shy and introverted. I didn't like being reserved, so to help myself feel better about this undesirable characteristic of my personality, I chose to just think of myself as quiet. I found a comfortable place in my life. I managed to center my world on music and band. All I wanted to think about was playing my French horn in marching and concert band. I enjoyed band practice and anything having to do with band, more than anything else. I dreamed about playing for the Symphony Orchestra one day. I was now in middle school, in the seventh grade. I was at such a delicate age. Just the thought of having to start over, make new friends and try to fit in well, simply overwhelmed me. I just remember crying incessantly. I don't even know who packed my clothes for me because I surely didn't. I totally lost my appetite, and I didn't get it back until days after we had been in California.

I was seriously beginning to realize that our father sometimes made important decisions on impulse, and that was not a healthy quality for one to possess. I also had another vital realization. I was young but strong, and I wasn't going to let this affect me negatively any longer. I had to learn to adjust to this new situation. I planned to get enrolled in the band program at the new school and try out for the performing band. After all, I did still have the same goals and aspirations. Also, if I didn't like anything about my personality, I had all of the control, and it was totally up to me to change it.

To my surprise, it only took about a week or so for me to adjust to being in California. I was actually making jokes about how much weight I lost by not eating. I couldn't help it. I had no appetite. I was amazed at how the mind can cause the body to react in this way. It reaffirmed my belief that if my frame of mind can cause my body to be sick, a positive change in my mindset can cause healing.

Aunt Noonie and Uncle Ben had moved their family including her parents, to San Jose. Now they all lived in the same house together on Fronda Drive. They bought a big beautiful Stucco home with a swimming pool in the back yard. They also had a gorgeous black and white Siberian husky with ice blue colored eyes named Duchess and a big beautiful German Shepherd named Duke. We started school right away. I went to Quimby Oak Middle School, and it was okay, I guess. I remember walking to and from school every day. I would not have thought that it would have been cold enough for coats in San Jose, California in the winter, yet I was wearing one. In fact, it was brand new. Aunt Noonie had just bought it for me.

So, while we were getting used to life in San Jose, Daddy went back to Huntsville to get guess who? Yes, he was bringing his friend, Ms. Baxter and her son back here with him this time. She put her house on the market, and they loaded up the truck, and they moved to Beverly... except it was San Jose.

They made it back safely, and Daddy brought them over to Uncle Ben and Aunt Noonie's house to meet everyone. It seemed to go well enough. Daddy rented an efficiency, and he stayed with Ms. Baxter and her son while he checked out the real estate market.

I don't remember how long they stayed there, but it wasn't long at all because they had not even enrolled her son in school, before she decided that she was unhappy here in San Jose and wanted to go back home to Alabama. Daddy said that the real estate was much too expensive here, and her reasoning was that she already had a house in Alabama that had not yet sold.

Daddy came to all of us and told us about his decision to move back to Huntsville. We couldn't believe it. I immediately turned toward my aunt and uncle and asked them if I could stay there in San Jose with them. Thank God, they said, "Yes, as long as it is okay with your father," but Daddy said no because he wanted to keep us together. I could not believe this was happening again. So, what do you think happened next?

"At any moment, the decision you make can change the course of your life forever."

Anthony Robbins

CHAPTER 3
My Teenage Years

The far distance between San Jose, CA and Huntsville, AL is approximately 2,300 miles. It took Daddy three days to drive back home, but that's because we stopped and stayed over at a motel each night. The days were long, and at least for me, the nights were sleepless. "Sunshine on My Shoulder" by John Denver, "Summer Breeze" and "Diamond Girl" by Seals and Croft are songs that were on the radio in the car. These and other songs in the same genre, helped get me through the long, gloomy, melancholy ride back to Alabama and would be forever embedded in my heart as favorites.

Once we made it there, the first thing Ms. Baxter and Daddy did was start making the necessary calls to get her house off of the market. For a while, we all lived at her house. I hated living there because I was in band, and she didn't appreciate the beautiful sound of the French horn. She actually made me practice on her back porch. I was not going to let her know it, but she hurt my feelings. It caused friction between us. I would never let her see me do it, but she actually made me cry. Ms. Baxter and I began to dislike each other, and to be honest, our relationship didn't improve until I was in my 40s.

We didn't live there for too long though because Daddy soon found a house of our own to move into on the North side of town. However, this didn't occur until he came in off of the road. You see, Daddy decided to drive a big truck for a while to make some extra income. He must have put his real estate career on hold.

This new house was in a different school district, which meant I wouldn't be attending the same high school as my friends from my middle school when the next school year began. All I could think of was that this was not fair, and life shouldn't have to be this hard for a girl my age. All I wanted was for things to stay the same, at least for a while. I didn't like change, and lately, everything was changing much too often. At least for now, since we were in the middle of the school year, I could go back to the same middle school and play with my familiar band members. It was now concert band season, my favorite time of the school year, and I didn't want anything to mess it up for me.

I was so glad to be moving into our own house because my walk home to her house was a dreaded, long uphill journey through the neighborhood behind my middle school, and I had a heavy French horn to carry home with me every day. Besides, the walk seemed to be causing my legs to feel strange. They felt heavy yet weak. I had not felt this before. It wasn't pain. It was more like discomfort. I assumed it was because of the two factors: the incline of the hills which was continuous and grew steeper with each block and the weight of the horn in the big case.

Being in our own house again was a welcomed feeling. Finally, we were able to cook food for ourselves and in our own kitchen. A negative though, was that we were back to eating foods that were not conducive to the healthiest diet. Since we were old enough to cook ourselves, my brother, sister and I would make just about whatever we had an appetite for, and it usually did not include any vegetables. In fact, our dinner was hardly ever a balanced meal.

Occasionally, Daddy would make his broiled chicken that he had become famous for in our eyes, but mostly, our palates craved for frozen pizza, ground beef patties or chili dogs with fries and my specialty, which was a patty melt on toast. We had a deep fryer, so we made shoestring French fries with just about everything. It wasn't very nutritious, but Daddy didn't ensure that we follow any nutritional guidelines for our meals when we would cook them ourselves. Of course, we still had invitations now and then, to have dinner at Daddy's friend Ms. Baxter's house.

The first day of high school for me was... to say the least, boring and discouraging. I wanted to be attending the rival school because that was where my friends from middle school would be going. In fact, I played hooky for the first couple of days. Daddy would leave the house first. So, when our carpool ride came, I just didn't go. Ms.

Baxter had a teenage sister, two nieces and a nephew who went to the same school. Her nephew had a car. Our house was on the way, so they just stopped and picked up me and my brother. Cynthia was still in middle school, so she left with Daddy. Peter finally told Daddy on me. Here I was at 15 years old, getting a whipping.

When I stopped rebelling, I began to focus on positive things like what classes were in my curriculum. Also, I was going to have to decide on what instrument to play in the band because the French horn that I played in middle school was only loaned to me. It was owned by the school. A French horn was much too expensive for Daddy to buy, so I decided to learn to play the clarinet. It was certainly going to be more challenging than the French horn because there were many more keys. Daddy purchased a clarinet for me. He paid for some initial lessons which were very helpful in getting me familiar with the instrument, the keys and reading the music. However, because of the expense, he couldn't afford very many.

I was really looking forward to marching band. In fact, I could hardly wait. I thought the band uniforms were quite distinctive. We were dressed like a general in the 1800s. It was a powder blue suit with a black bow tie and a floppy white brim hat.

Actually, there was another uniform that I would love to have worn. It was the uniform of the "Confederettes." I was such a girly-girl, and I had a secret aspiration of being on the high school dance team. I never shared this with anyone, not even my own sister or my closest friends. I wouldn't even think of trying out for the team. I didn't even know if Daddy would let me be one if I made it because he was so strict. My father kept us on a pretty tight rein, especially me and Cynthia. Besides, I knew that I had poor balance and coordination. For these reasons, I probably wouldn't have been a good candidate because of the difficult dance routines. I thought that I probably should just stick to learning marching band formations.

I do recall times when I felt the need to carefully pay attention to the bleachers or the steps at the football stadium, when the band would leave from or return to our seats. I often felt as if I could very easily trip up and fall or something. Also, I do remember that walking on the graveled areas around the stadium was sometimes a bit challenging. I noticed it but didn't put hardly any thought into it because it really wasn't that much of an issue.

I was learning a new instrument. So, I was not nearly as good as the other members who had been playing their instruments for a long time. It was ironic because I played by ear, which meant I played without sheet music. I could hear a song on the radio, remember it and teach myself how to play it with little effort. However, I wasn't very good at reading music, which is a skill that is necessary in order to perform well in band. Nevertheless, band was a very important part of my life.

Our high school band traveled quite often, performing in various competitions and even some professional halftime shows. We were in Jimmy Carter's Inaugural Parade in Washington D.C. in 1977. I traveled with the band to St. Louis, Missouri and New Orleans, Louisiana. I went to several nice places, met some quite interesting people and created many unforgettable experiences which I will always remember. In fact, I recently reconnected with a pen pal who I met on my high school St. Louis band trip. We kept in touch. He is the owner and leader of an R&B band in San Antonio, Texas. He plays base.

There was one particular band trip which I wasn't able to attend. I missed out on this one, and my dad was to blame. Honestly, I wasn't able to forgive him until I was near 40, believe it or not. Our marching band was going to Dallas or Houston, Texas for a competition. My band director arranged for a uniform to be altered at no charge to me. I attended all of the band practices. So, I learned the formations, and of course, all of the music. All Daddy was responsible for was paying for my meals for the weekend. It would have been less than 20 dollars. On the morning that we were departing, Daddy still hadn't said anything to me about whether or not I was able to go. It was obvious that he wasn't able to afford to give me any money for my meals, yet he refused to discuss it with me. Therefore, I never showed up at the school, and the band bus left without me.

The following Monday when I showed up for band period, my band director seemed upset with me, to say the least. Obviously, I knew and understood exactly why. He immediately and quickly walked me to the counselor's office to change my schedule, moving me back to the intermediate band from the advanced band. I completely empathized with him because my absence probably messed up the formation. Even so, my feelings were hurt very badly because it wasn't my fault. I was a very sensitive kid. He would never know it, but it actually made me cry. I wanted to apologize to our band director, but even if the opportunity presented itself, I guess I never got up enough nerve to actually do it.

We moved one last time before I graduated from high school. Before the move, Peter quit school in the 10th grade and joined the US Armed Forces. He went to the army and was stationed in Germany. So, Cynthia and I finally had our own rooms. The house was a yellow brick ranch with dark brown shutters, a garage and a huge backyard.

Our dog loved having all of this open space in which to run around and play. When Peter was here, someone gave him a cute little German Shepherd puppy. He named him Duke because he reminded us of Aunt Noonie, Uncle Ben and our cousin's dog in California, named Duke.

We lived here in this house longer than any of the others. Daddy was renting from a friend of his who owned the house. We lived there for four or five years. Daddy's bedroom and bathroom was on one end of the house. Cynthia and I had bedrooms on the other end, and we shared a bathroom. The living room was at the front of the house, and the den and kitchen blended together like one large space in the middle of the house. The den had a sliding glass door which enabled us to view the entire backyard. The house sat on top of a hill. So, the end of our yard was at the bottom of the hill.

This yard was just perfect for our large German Shepherd. He even had a little island with a tree and a couple of bushes which gave him the perfect amount of shade. In the winter or when it rained, I guess he slept under the house in the crawl space. This explained why he had the red mud on his fur that we had to occasionally wash off by giving him a bath.

Most teenagers that I knew, started dating in high school, but Daddy would only allow me to talk to a boy on the telephone. I had crushes on a couple of them. He was okay with it unless he heard me giggling on the phone when it was getting close to 10:00 PM. Well, this was usually the case because 10 came around pretty quickly, especially if I was really into him or thought he was cute and fine. I would hear Daddy's bare feet pacing back and forth on the kitchen floor on the other side of my closed bedroom door. This was my warning. I knew that if I didn't hang up the phone right then, he was going to embarrass me by saying something that would make me look like a child to the boy on the other end of the phone. I wasn't about to let that happen. So, I would just say to him, "I'll check you later" in my big girl's voice and get off of the phone.

I was now 17 and a sophomore. I was "talking" to this boy. That's what we called it back in the 70s when you were involved with someone but not necessarily officially dating them. When you were "talking" to someone, it could mean that you were engaging in telephone conversations only. This was definitely, always the case for me because my sister and I were not yet allowed to go out with boys. In fact, Daddy never did open that door for us. So, we could only see each other at school. It was there that we could walk through the hallways with his arm around me, hold hands or maybe steal a sweet kiss at the locker.

His name was Franklin. He invited me over to his mom's house for Christmas dinner once, and Daddy actually let me buy a gift for him. In those days, we had to have our father's permission before doing almost anything. I remember the time that my brother gave a girl a necklace. When Daddy became aware of it, he made Peter get it back and return it to the store. Poor Peter was so embarrassed. So, to keep any craziness such as that from happening to myself, I asked him first.

Anyway, my gift was a handsome taupe sweater that I bought on sale for 19 dollars. I found it at London Transit. It was a popular men's store at Loveman's Mall. I really didn't think Daddy would let me go, but he surprised me and was actually fine with it.

After dinner, Franklin's mom gave him the keys to her brand-new car and said we could use it for the evening. We took it up to Monte Sano. It's a state park in Huntsville. At night, it was the spot for couples to drive their vehicles up on the mountain, park under the stars, and I guess if they wanted to... some people would make out.

One evening, I got up the nerve to do something really bold and daring. I knew that Daddy was at the pool room and would be for a pretty good while. So, Franklin and I decided that he was going to come and pick me up without Daddy knowing about it. We were going to the movie theater. I can't remember what movie we saw, but I swore Cynthia to secrecy.

When the movie was over and he brought me back home, he started playing around, driving back and forth past my house, but he wouldn't stop and let me out. He was laughing, but I didn't see anything funny about it because if Daddy beat me home and I wasn't already in the house, I would be in for it. Daddy would probably go to jail for attempting to murder his teenage daughter. What we were doing was so risky. I was scared out of my mind, and he just kept driving around as if we had all of the time in the world. I just knew that I was going to get caught.

When he finally let me out of the car, I slammed the door shut and without saying a word to him, went inside... thanking Jesus that Daddy did not pull up first. Needless to say, I learned my lesson that day and was never tempted to sneak out again.

My sister and I were growing up. We were "Good girls," but it was normal that we were becoming a little inquisitive about the topic of sex. Of course, there was Home Economics class which addressed some sex education. Obviously, we couldn't ask Daddy anything. That would be out of the question. He would have made us wear a chastity belt if he knew that we were at all curious about that subject. A classmate and neighbor who lived down the street, was sexually active. She didn't mind, in fact, she loved telling us about her encounters. She was very detailed and descriptive, and if we had any questions about the intimate act, she was more than willing to share her experiences with us. She would even illustrate.

I cannot really remember, and don't ask me exactly how, but I think she even demonstrated how to kiss a boy using her hand. Back then, we thought she was quite hilarious. So, we paid attention to her because she was entertaining. However, I didn't have that same mindset, and I was not an impressionable young lady. So, even though he didn't know we were showing an interest in this, Daddy had nothing to worry about, yet.

Thinking back to that time, it is disheartening that a young girl that age would have so much of that type of experience. I never saw her or heard anything about her after high school, except that she worked at the local K-mart. I wonder how her life turned out. I pray that it is blessed.

Now, it was around this time that I heard from a dear friend of mine. We had somehow lost touch with each other during our freshman year. I had known her since elementary school, and she had a disability. Her right lower extremity was smaller and much weaker due to a childhood illness.

I always admired her strength and tenacity. Even back when we were kids, she did everything that the other kids did, and some things she did better. She had so much determination. We rode bicycles together, regardless of the fact that she was wearing a full metal brace on her leg with leather straps. It was attached to a shoe with an elevated sole. I admired her so much for having such a strong will. It was so good to hear from her. She had transferred to the rival high school, the one where I wanted to attend.

She was now planning her wedding. She was going to be a very young bride. However, when you're in love and you know or even think you have found your soulmate, age doesn't matter, right? She asked me if I would be one of her two bridesmaids. I accepted graciously and was very honored. It was such a beautiful wedding. She was 17 and they are still happily married today. They have three adult children and several grandchildren.

I feel like God placed this beautiful soul who just happened to have this disability, in my life because He knew my future. He wanted her to be a part of my inspiration. No matter what different paths God chooses our lives to take us, in my heart she will always be one of my dearest friends.

Music has always been a constant interest in my life. I love both vocal and instrumental sounds of various genres. So, when the Von Braun Civic Center was built in Huntsville in March of 1975, I began my concert going experiences.

My first R&B concert was Frankie Beverly & Maze. It was at this concert that I learned the importance of arriving a couple of hours earlier than everyone else, to ensure that I would get the idealistic spot for the ultimate view of the performing artist.

My second concert was a very young... Prince. He was 20 years old when he was on tour, promoting his debut album, *For You* with the hit single "Soft and Wet." I, as well as probably every other Prince fan in Huntsville and the surrounding areas, awoke this particular morning feeling totally pumped up and overly anxious to see and hear the R&B artist, Prince. He and his band would be performing at the Von Braun Civic Center that evening.

Music lovers all over town like myself, had finally received in the civic center what we never before had the opportunity to experience. We now had an all-purpose facility, constructed to accommodate concerts, Broadway show performances, ballets, symphonies and a full variety of sporting events, right here in our own city.

At school, this concert was all we had been talking about. It was going to be one of the most highly anticipated events that Huntsville had seen and for myself, the experience of a lifetime. So, Daddy dropped me off and would pick me up in the same place. I always seemed to attend the concerts all by myself, but that was always fine with me because I was somewhat of a loner anyway. Besides, this way I wouldn't ruin anyone else's good time if I needed to stop and sit down or if my legs were to feel as if they were going to give out or something crazy like that. At least this is what I would tell myself in order to not feel so obviously different. I didn't understand why my legs were curiously unpredictable sometimes. It seemed to have always been that way.

Anyhow without delay, I made it inside, presented my ticket and proceeded to the concert arena. Since, I had already pre-determined exactly where I needed to go, based on exactly where I wanted to be when the concert began, I headed toward the floor and front and center of the stage. Security had the area closest to the stage chained off, but I had my radar focused on it because that was where I was going to stand, dance and enjoy the show for the entire night. I was relieved. I could now relax and just breathe because I had arrived. I was going to have the best possible standing spot in the house. I would be right at the stage, in front of Prince. I couldn't be any higher than I was, on cloud number nine.

The downfall was that by the end of the night my legs felt very strained, both heavy and weak at the same time. This was a feeling that was beginning to become all too familiar and happening much too frequently.

My very first Prince experience will definitely always be cherished, especially since "The Purple One" is no longer with us. Candidly, it was one of the most special performances I have ever seen. I know I saw other artists perform at the Von Braun, like Maze and Slave with their hit "Slide," but the Prince concert stands out in my mind as my favorite because I honestly cannot even name or for that matter, think of any other band that was as good. Honestly, I would really have to search my memory bank to even try and come up with one.

In addition to music, I was fascinated by writing. I would put short stories on paper, never intending to do anything with them. I just wanted to let them out of my head.

Another one of my hobbies was cooking, baking in particular. I liked making cakes, cookies and one particular pie, lemon ice box. The cake that I had the most success with was either a one or two layered spice cake with a butter-creme frosting, and I loved baking chocolate chip and oatmeal -n- raisin cookies. The thing is that none of the recipes were from scratch. In fact, the cake and the chocolate chip cookies were both made from a popular boxed cake mix, but I did get the oatmeal cookie recipe from the top of the oatmeal box. Nevertheless, this interest in an attempt to bake, led to my real interest in baking. I make a really good sweet potato pie, pecan pie and red velvet cake.

My brother used to make doughnuts. His recipe was to roll a biscuit out, use a cookie cutter to cut a hole out of the center and deep fry it. It will puff up into a doughnut. Shake it in powdered sugar, sprinkle sugared cinnamon on it or frost the top of it with chocolate, vanilla or strawberry frosting. Add nuts or sprinkles if you have kids and there you go... home-made doughnuts. They melt in your mouth. By the way, my brother would fry the doughnuts, but my sister and I put the yummy stuff on them. I was given an easy recipe for lemon icebox pie, but I might tell you more about that later.

Now, one memory that I unfortunately do not have is that of prom night because strangely enough, I did not attend nor did I attend any of the school dances. I would tell myself that it was because I was too shy, and that was probably part of the reason, but there was another reason which once revealed will make better sense.

It was that time of the year again. This time it was my Senior Class preparing for the prom. The theme was "Too Much Heaven."

This happened to be one of my favorite songs by The Bee Gees.

Though, I was asked by a certain boy in my Senior Class, I didn't attend my prom. I told him, "Thank you but I'm not going," before I even thought about it. You see, the fact was that I did want to go, but there were two strikes against me going. The first was that I was painfully shy. However, that hurdle, I could have gotten over if I had really wanted to because my desire to attend was greater than whatever it was that I thought I was afraid of... Just the idea of buying the new dress, shoes and going to a salon for nails, hair, and make-up, seemed so glamorous and like so much fun. So, what was stopping me? It was because I knew that I had two left feet. The matter went back to my having a problem with lack of coordination. Therefore, I had no self-confidence at all in regard to dancing. I remember feeling like I just couldn't go. Therefore, I didn't, and it was my loss. I deeply regret not going to my Senior Prom, and looking back, I sincerely wish I had felt confident enough to accept Nelson's offer.

So, my daddy started attending a Presbyterian church and joined their congregation. He rededicated his life to Christ and was making a lot of friends within the church.

One day, Daddy had a terrible accident in the backyard. The grass was damp because it had been raining the day before. Still, Daddy decided to cut the grass. The yard was large and had a steep hill. While he was cutting on the hill, his foot slipped under the part of the mower that concealed the blade. The blade cut into the end of his sneaker where his toes were located. He quickly came into the house and without telling us what happened, went straight to the garage, got into his car and drove himself to the emergency room. After removing his sneaker, the doctor determined that the tips of his toes had been cut off. Some were reattached. However, in an attempt to save the toes, he would have to keep his foot elevated for weeks, in hopes of getting the blood to start circulating again.

The next few weeks were difficult for me because I never saw a time when my father was sick or unable to work or function normally. I remember it being very hard for me to maintain my schoolwork. As a matter of fact, I did not want to even go.

While he was confined to the bed, friends from his church would drop by to visit him frequently. However, I noticed that his friend, Ms. Baxter, never came over. Eventually, he told us that they would no longer be seeing each other because their relationship did not glorify God. Later, she would confirm what he told us. She said although she still loved him, she wasn't ready to suddenly become "All religious" overnight.

I was actually witnessing a really profound transformation taking place within my father. He was choosing God, and it was a phenomenal change to observe.

Though I held quite a few jobs at various fast food restaurants during my junior and senior year, my first job was at a florist shop through a school work study program. The fast food restaurants were Taco Bell and Wendy's, which was a brand-new hamburger restaurant named after the founder's daughter. I was also, part of a team that opened Wiener King. It was a new hot dog franchise in Huntsville. Unfortunately, it was not a hit, and it closed in one year.

However, my most favorite teenage employment experience was with Baskin Robbins Ice Cream. I will never forget it. I was 17, and I worked with the greatest group of people. I've reconnected with some of them. We still keep in contact through social media. We had the best of times at work.

There were a few loyal customers who we called friends, that came in even during the winter months for conversation, coffee or even a Hot Fudge sundae.

Marvin was a homeless man who pushed a grocery basket filled with junk that he picked up on the street. He would come in, and we would give him a cup of ice water if it was hot outside. However, if our manager wasn't there, we would offer him a cup of coffee or a scoop of ice cream. She did not want us to give him anything for free because she said that it would encourage him to hang around.

One summer day while at work, a teenaged couple came into the ice cream parlor. They were a cute couple, laughing and lovingly playing with each other. I recognized the girl. She was Maureen from my high school, and she also lived in my neighborhood. I didn't know her boyfriend, but he was the most beautiful boy I had ever seen in my entire life. I remember feeling kind of envious and thinking to myself that she was so lucky. They stopped giggling just long enough to order some ice cream, then they left just as quickly as they came.

Oddly enough, I couldn't get my mind off of him. In fact, I thought about him for the rest of the day. I worked at Baskin-Robbins during the entire summer break after my senior year and throughout my freshman and sophomore years of college.

Daddy was taking me to work one day, when I noticed a vehicle parked in the grass on North Memorial Parkway with for sale signs on the front and side windows. It was a 1969 Chevelle-Malibu with a gold matte finish. I pointed it out to Daddy, and he said he would go back and look at it after he dropped me off. So, I told him where to find the money which I was saving. It was in my bedroom at the house. I had it hidden in a special place. Although I knew it should have been in the bank. When he picked me up at the end of my shift, he said he had taken it to an auto-mechanic, and it was in excellent condition. The best part was that the owner sold it to him for only 275 dollars. It had black leather seats, and they were in perfect condition. It had a good working heater. Unfortunately, there was no air conditioner. I was young and happy just to have my own car, so I could live with that imperfection.

Daddy was always there for us when we needed him to be. He bought a car for Peter when he turned 16. It was a nice used red Oldsmobile with a black top. I don't know what year it was, but it sure was pretty. However, he took it back when he saw the car parked at a local housing project one time too many. Peter had become friends with Daddy's friend's nephews, and they lived in this housing project, but honestly, Peter would not have known them if it weren't for Daddy's association with Ms. Baxter and her family, right? Whose fault was this? Not my brother's.

He took Cynthia to a used car dealership one day, and she bought her first car before she left for college at the University of North Alabama in Florence. She would now be responsible for making car payments.

I was pleased that I was responsible for getting my own as well. Although, I did take a lot of pride in being very independent, I appreciated him negotiating this automobile transaction for me. I drove my car for 2 1/2 years, then I traded it. I only did this because a semi-tractor trailer truck hit me and messed up the front left fender.

I was waiting for traffic, getting ready to turn onto North Memorial Parkway from the Hardees parking lot when the large rig failed to turn widely enough. His trailer bed actually went over my hood. I thought I was going to be beheaded. He left the scene, and I only had liability insurance. Well, I no longer wanted to drive the car damaged, so I traded it (but it was later during college when this incident happened).

Graduation day was finally here, and it was time for me to receive my much highly-deserved academic degree at my high school's commencement. Aunt Noonie and Uncle Ben flew in from San Jose, California. For them to come all of the way over here... well it made me feel so special and loved. All of the attention that I was receiving today was delightful. Today, the Merritt's were celebrating me, and to say that I was floating on air, was an understatement. We were really, truly having a "Fun family now." My graduation would be at the Von Braun Civic Center.

The school's yearbook photographer was taking random pictures of us. Later, I would see a picture of myself in the yearbook wearing my cap-n-gown. I wasn't smiling. The pages were reflecting our graduation day. The captions were, "The smiles" and under my pic it read, "And the tears."

It seemed as if we had been waiting in line forever. Finally, we were given our signal to proceed into the big hall. The ceremony was about to begin, and we were all so very excited. However, I was also feeling anxious.

The hall was filled with the many families and friends of all of the graduating students. The principal, guidance counselors, teachers and speakers were present as well. After all of the speeches and recognitions had been given, they were finally ready for us to walk across the stage and receive our diplomas. This exercise was accomplished in alphabetical order. Then promptly, after the class valedictorian spoke, the principal said his final words, and we threw our caps up in the air. The music began, and after everyone hugged and cried, we proceeded to walk out. I took pictures outside with my family. I cannot really remember them taking me out to some nice restaurant to eat, so I guess we just headed back to the house for dinner.

It wasn't God's intention for Daddy to be alone because He soon gave him his Ruth. Daddy and Lula Hammonds met one Saturday when he visited the Oakwood Seventh Day Adventist Church and College. They began having conversations on the phone which led to their studying the Holy Bible together. They were accountability partners and kept each other lifted up. Daddy finished Seminary, and Lula wanted to go, so Daddy tutored her. They became prayer partners. They prayed for each other weekly, daily and sometimes, hourly. They were best friends and a while later, man and wife. In fact, it was only a few months later when they realized, God had sent them to each other. It is because they both have given me their own personal account of their union, that I am cognizant of these details.

It happened when my senior year ended and before my college freshman year began. We were totally unaware of their involvement with each other. As I recall, we were riding in our green Chrysler New Yorker with Daddy one day, when he said to us, "Well, your father is a married man now." Cynthia and I looked at each other in shock... to put it mildly, and both of us said at the same time, "To who"?

Daddy refreshed our memories by reminding us that we spent a couple of nights with her and her two boys once, when he had some business out of town. Immediately, we knew who he was talking about. Our father was beginning a new chapter in his life, and it seemed as if he was doing this without even involving us... at all. Maybe he felt as though his children were embarking on their own new journeys, and he wasn't about to be left all by himself.

"Being a Teenager was one of the hardest things I've ever done. However, it molded me into the strong person, I am today."

Shirley A. Merritt

CHAPTER 4
Alabama A&M

It was time for me to figure out exactly what it was that I wanted to do in life and where I wanted to go in order to develop the knowledge for a career. I was thinking a lot about modeling and how rewarding and glamorous a career in this industry would be but then I was so shy, not to mention, very short. I figured, maybe this would be the career that could help me to develop personality and some much needed, self-confidence.

Now, being ambitious, yet introverted did not really fit together. Sometimes, I had the desire to do something but not the courage. I knew I wasn't tall enough for Runway modeling. However, after calling and speaking with a representative at the Barbizon Modeling Agency in Atlanta, Georgia, I was encouraged to consider Studio modeling, which could include Catalog modeling. It was a smaller industry, and the challenge was... providing enough work for the models to make a sufficient income. The modeling industry wasn't like it is today, where models of any size, age, or ethnic background are welcomed. They also mentioned Petite modeling. They wanted to make an appointment with me and my parents to come and tour their facility. I decided to bring the subject up to Daddy for a discussion. He did not seem to be very convinced that my career choice was a good one, and he wouldn't give me his permission to schedule the interview appointment with the school. In fact, he never even brought up the subject again.

I knew my daddy, and if he did not buy into something or see eye to eye with you on it, he would simply avoid talking to you about it. He wouldn't bring it up at all, which made me rather hesitant about initiating any more conversation about my sudden interest. I was disappointed because this meant that he was more than likely, closing the door on any further discussions about what he probably felt was my impulsive desire to become a model. I wasn't going to debate my career choice with him. Since I needed his financial support for my education, I decided to put my modeling career aspirations on the back burner, at least for now. So, I began to give college some careful consideration.

I was looking at the University of Huntsville (UAH) and was also interested in the University of Alabama in Tuscaloosa, Alabama. My stepmother graduated from Alabama A&M University in Normal, Alabama, which was just down the street from us, on Meridian. She suggested that I might give her Alma Mater some careful thought. However, I was favoring Alabama Crimson Tide. Summer break was starting, and it would soon be September. The fall semester would begin shortly. Daddy recommended that I attend A&M in my freshman year. Then if I still wanted to go, I could transfer to the University of Alabama in my sophomore year. So, I agreed and decided to give the Bulldogs a try.

I recently started relaxing my own hair and did a pretty good job, but I decided to go to the beauty shop and get it done this time because it isn't every day that you start college. Besides, I wanted to have it cut in layers. When the beautician finished her work of art and put the mirror in my hands, I absolutely loved it. It was a cute, smart cut with long layers on the top and the sides. She cut it shoulder length in the back. I could hardly wait to show off my new hairstyle. I knew of several students from my high school who were planning on attending the same college. Who would have thought that getting a new hairdo would give me such a boost of self-confidence? I was beginning to get excited about going to A&M, after all. Now, if I could only get half as excited about starting the classes.

(AAMU) represents the Alabama Agricultural and Mechanical University. It is a historically Black institution and one of the first Land-Grant Colleges, founded by a former slave named William Hooper Council. It opened in 1875 with only 61 students and two teachers. Today, Alabama A&M is known throughout the world and has various cultures within the student body.

Since my most recent fascination of pursuing a career in the modeling and fashion industry did not turn out well, I chose fashion merchandising to be my major with a concentration in marketing. I figured this career might be the next best thing. What I didn't know then but I surely learned after I earned the degree was that certainly, a model can have a somewhat quiet personality; however, a merchandiser/buyer has to be very assertive, and that wasn't one of my greatest strengths.

I decided to reside at home throughout my freshman year. The long registration and financial aid lines were the worst part of the enrollment process for the upcoming school year. The wait lines seemed endless, but it was worth it because after everything was processed and the tuition fees were all paid, the grant recipients received highly anticipated grant refund checks. I used my refund for my first set of soft contact lenses. Finally, I was going to be able to remove these eye glasses, and this was happening right before I began this new adventure in my life. My contacts were 250 dollars.

The campus was nicknamed "The Hill" because it was actually on a hill, which did not make it easy at all to walk from one building to another when changing classes. There were times when I had a class at the bottom of the hill and had to be at the top for a class the next hour. As if that weren't enough, I did this while wearing high heels every day. That's right, super straight legged, faded blue jeans were the fashion style for the ladies on campus, and we wore them without a belt and with a dressy blouse tucked inside. Then we accessorized the look with a pair of stylish stilettos or high heeled pumps. I remember walking up and down the sidewalks of those hills. Interestingly enough, I always looked down at my feet. I was carefully calculating my steps. I was doing this for two reasons. One was to keep my heels from landing in the cracks of the sidewalk and scarring them up, and the other was to keep from losing my balance. I didn't know why, but this happened quite frequently. It was so strange, and I couldn't figure it out.

Daddy and Lula moved away to her hometown of Birmingham, Alabama, where they started an inner-city children's ministry. They named their ministry El Shaddai, which translates as God Almighty. Peter had been discharged from the Army and was now living back in Huntsville. He was earning an electronics degree at Drake Technical College. Cynthia and her yellow Ventura went off to college at the University of North Alabama (UNA) in Florence, Alabama, and I moved on campus in my sophomore year.

I lived in a dormitory named Thigpen Hall. My roommate and I became pretty good friends, and we had mutual friends. She was from a small town in Mississippi. Our dormitory was a residence hall for women, named after the educator-Emily Thigpen. There were only about four women's dorms and three men's dorms in all, when I attended back in 1979-83.

Most of the students had meal cards. They elected to eat in the cafeteria. I was trying to have as few expenses as possible. Since my tuition was being paid solely by an Educational Grant, I chose to forego the meal card. Don't ask me how I ate on a regular basis because honestly, I do not remember. I still worked part time at Baskin Robbins, so I suppose I just ate off campus a lot, and there were many nights when dinner was a Hot Fudge or Caramel sundae with nuts, a Hot Fudge Brownie Delight or a Banana Royale with whipped cream. I was very tiny and could eat just about anything I wanted, without gaining weight.

We had a few different nicknames for the A&M campus. As I already mentioned, there was "The Hill." We also called it "The Yard," and there was an area outside of "The Caf" (which was short for the cafeteria) and the Student Union building, where a lot of the students would congregate in between classes. It was the gathering spot after lunch and dinner or in the evenings, just to hang out. We called it "The Block." One day, while I was on "The Block" with some friends, a couple of guys in suits approached me and told me that they noticed me. The GQ look was in, and some of the guys actually wore suits and ties on campus. They went on about how they were observing me, and they admired the way in which I carried myself. They asked me if I would be interested in becoming a Kappa Alpha

Psi Sweetheart. After talking with them further about it and getting more details, I was flattered and decided that yes, I was indeed interested in having this title and being a part of their organization. Later, they informed me that my title was Miss Pi, of Phi Nu Pi. Phi Nu Pi is a secret expression or motto of this fraternity. They also have a secret handshake. The Kappa Alpha Psi Fraternity was founded in 1911. It was one of the very first African-American fraternities. The role of the Sweetheart is to aid and support the members in various service and social statuses. They provide direction for the fraternity brothers of their respective chapter. The Sweethearts also acted as hostesses for their chapter's events.

We were celebrating the Christmas holiday season, and the Kappa Sweethearts were in the Christmas parade in downtown Huntsville. We were sitting on a cream-colored convertible, all dressed up in cream suits with red blouses. We were representing the Kappa Alpha Psi Fraternity at Alabama A&M. I felt as if I was on top of the world, and I loved the attention we were getting as we waved to the crowd with gloves on our hands to keep them warm.

Huntsville had just recently completed many renovations on the downtown area, so the winter ambiance with all of the decorations was absolutely breathtaking. I remember feeling like that Barbizon fashion model.

It was my sophomore year when I met him, talked to him and started dating "That fine dude." This is what I called him because before I met him, I did not know his name for over a year. I first noticed him in my freshman year, but he had a girlfriend then, and I never saw him without her. They seemed inseparable and like they were so much in love or something. It was one of the very few times I had eaten in "The Caf", when he noticed me. I was sitting with my roommate, eating whatever they served us for lunch that day. He walked over and slid his food tray onto our table, then he kind of just rudely sat down in front of me. I didn't mind at all though because I wanted to meet him, but I didn't anticipate that we ever would.

He was from Gulf Shores, Alabama. He was not gorgeous, but I did think he was very cute. He wore a shag haircut. You know, that was the popular style worn by the guys who were transitioning from the Afro, but they were having a hard time letting it go. He had a light caramel brown complexion with a dimple on each cheek, a very defined jawline and a long perfectly chiseled nose, as well as a long-waist and a very fit torso. What I always noticed about him was his nice physique. I thought he was so fine. He always wore these fitted, faded, tapered legged blue jeans that outlined the shape of his calves. He wore white sneakers, and his shirt tail was always out. Anyway... earth to Shirley because I now had his attention, and Tyler already had mine. In fact, we kept each other's attention for the next seven years of our lives. Oh, did I mention that he was really wearing those jeans?

I needed a source of income while I was in school, so I kept my part-time job at Baskin Robbins. Be that as it may, Daddy wasn't providing me with any financial support. I think that in his mind, he thought that my being away in college meant that I was totally on my own. Anyhow, I enjoyed working there, and I wasn't ready to give it up just yet.

Working a part time job, being a full-time student and now somebody's girlfriend, was leaving me with not a lot of time for anything else, and in my mind, that included studying. Let's just say that I was easily distracted, and I did have a couple of diversions. I should have been more disciplined to have better study habits, then maybe I would have made better grades. They weren't poor by any means, but they weren't as good as they should have been either.

At the ice cream parlor, we were allowed to have free ice cream treats and fountain drinks during our shift. So, sometimes I would bring my boyfriend Tyler, a Hot Fudge sundae made with his favorite, French vanilla ice cream.

I worked the evening and night shifts. So, I always closed the store, except for on the weekends when I might be scheduled for a day shift. By the time I made it back to the campus all of the parking spaces behind Thigpen Hall were taken. There were not that many for some strange reason. I found a spot about 30 or so feet down the hill behind my dorm, and it was always available. It was as if God made that special spot just for me and my Chevelle Malibu. However, once I parked, I had to climb back up the hill in order to get into a back door of my dorm.

When I look back at the things that I was willing and able to do in my youth, I am kind of amazed sometimes. Young people just don't think that many things are too difficult for them. Maybe it is because they put so much value on having their independence. Furthermore, if something is hard on them, they tend to make the best of it. I think that is exactly what I was doing. My siblings and I lived such a sheltered life when we were under Daddy's roof that we were so much more than ready to spread our wings and fly... totally on our own. Even when we faced obstacles, we never really had Daddy to run to because he started a new life for himself, and he just wasn't there for us in that way anymore. However, he could feel extremely confident in knowing that he had raised two very strong, independent and enabling daughters who loved him dearly and were grateful to him for being such a good example of these positive characteristics. I owe the development of my adamant persistence and determination, which are my strengths, to my father because I first saw these attributes in him.

My big brother, Peter, had been renting a room from his friends. They were a married couple who had two small children, and they had another extra room that they wanted to rent to someone else. He asked me if I knew about anyone who might be interested. I immediately thought about renting it for myself and didn't hesitate to tell him that yes in fact, I was interested. Living on campus was good, but my roommate had been acting antisocial toward me once again, and to say that I was beginning to grow tired of her antics and mood swings was an understatement. She was uncommunicative, avoidant and just downright unfriendly toward me, and I'd had enough of it! I hoped that she would talk to me about whatever it was that was bothering her, but I realized that this was something that probably was just not going to happen. I didn't know if she was what we now call being bipolar, depressed or maybe just suffering from premenstrual syndrome (PMS). After all, mood swings are considered to be normal behavior, but when emotions become extreme and obsessive, it might be that they are indicative of some hidden ailment.

I decided to keep my plans to myself. At the end of the semester when everyone else including Olivia was packing up to go home for the Christmas break, I was putting away my belongings to leave the dorm for good. I was a good friend, and I had not knowingly done anything to deserve this silent treatment that she was giving me. The thing is that, this wasn't the first time, but it would definitely be the last time. I really didn't want to handle it this way. However, it almost seemed necessary. I honestly believed this to be the best way. She was going to be surprised when she returned after the break because my side of the room would be empty. Don't get me wrong. I was going to miss living in Thigpen Hall. I had friends there, and we did have some memorable times. Some of my most treasured R&B records will always remind me of those days and nights when I lived in the dorm at A&M. Records like "I'm Ready" by Kano, "Push" by Brick, "Stomp" by The Brother's Johnson and "It's a love thing" by The Whispers, take me back there to 1980. Above all, it was my first experience at living away from Daddy.

I was really enjoying living off-campus. I was getting first-hand experience at paying rent and some other bills and expenses that I didn't have when I was living in the dorm. So, I was truly feeling my newly established independence, and I was loving it, as well as the anticipation of receiving an increased grant refund check.

It was the beginning of summer break, and Tyler was doing an internship in Detroit. His major was in engineering. He had become a constant in my life. Although I looked forward to the summer months ahead... I was also, very anxiously awaiting his return to Huntsville in the fall. Now my brother and I only saw this living arrangement as a very temporary situation. I believe that by letting me move in and rent this room with him and these people, he was just ensuring that I was well protected and safe. This was his way of looking out for his little sis because he quickly found another apartment for us, and we moved out.

We chose to move into a duplex apartment and rented our furniture. It was an older small brick ranch. We had not been living there for very long at all when a fire broke out in the other unit, and sadly, we lost everything. It was okay though because we had each other, and we were both unharmed. In fact, I was working the night it happened. What's more, at our very young ages, we had not yet acquired many possessions. The funny thing was, even though back then, we didn't think it was so funny, when we called Daddy to let him know what happened and that we lost everything we owned, he simply gave us his well wishes and said he would pray for us. Go figure. Now, I know prayer means everything but still...

Daddy's ex-friend Ms. Baxter, let us stay in her home while we were looking for another place to live. To our advantage, we found one right away. This one was a new apartment development. There were about a dozen of nice newly built buildings on one street. Each building had four units. There were two on the ground level and two upstairs. Each upstairs unit had a separate staircase leading directly up to the front door. We chose to rent one of the upstairs units. The apartment had two bedrooms and two bathrooms. We also had a washer and dryer. It was exactly what we wanted. Again, we rented all of our furniture... two-bedroom sets, a living room and a dining room set.

It was the most idealistic little apartment, and I could hardly wait for Tyler to see it when he returned for the new school year. Dating each other was going to be so different and so much fun, now that I was no longer living on campus. I needed to change my criterion for my study practices. Tyler and his friends were actually, scholarly students. Anyhow, there would be no strict dormitory rules to follow. We affectionately referred to each other as eating buddies already. So, now we would be able to cook and eat together as well as, come and go as we pleased. We weren't going to know what to do with all of this unfamiliar freedom. I knew that establishing and maintaining good study habits for myself was going to be more than challenging. In fact, it was going to be quite difficult.

Now that we had our new place, Cynthia would come from UNA and stay for the weekend sometimes. Me, my Malibu and usually one of my girlfriends, would take an occasional road trip to Florence and visit her as well. My sister was really enjoying college life and living on campus. She was dating a Kappa, and she was also Greek. She had pledged the Delta Sigma Theta Sorority. Coincidently, the colors of each Fraternity and Sorority are crimson and cream. We enjoyed touring the campus and meeting her friends. Cynthia would fascinate us with her stories about why they all believed that the mezzanine in their dormitory was haunted. She amused us when she told us about how she lived off of eating popcorn and diet coke so that she could maintain her cute and shapely figure. However, on a more serious note, she intrigued us when she shared an article that she read about a woman who was diagnosed with an illness called multiple sclerosis. After giving birth, she was unable to hold and care for her baby because her arms were suddenly so very weak. Also, she almost immediately and unexpectedly became wheelchair bound. She felt so much empathy for this woman because this disease had suddenly robbed the mother of her normal and busy life. To my sister, this condition was one of the most devastating that she had ever heard about. I remember... we listened intently. For some reason, she definitely had our attention.

For several months, everything was really good at Lake Park Apartments. Tyler was coming over for dinner quite often, and I was becoming a fabulous cook. He loved my baked chicken, and my spaghetti was also one of his favorites. We were able to watch TV and even study together. He was so glad to be able to escape and get away from his dorm and the university. Sometimes, I would wash his hair and oil his scalp for him. We had the best long and most meaningful conversations. We would talk about any and everything. I could share my deepest and most private thoughts with him. On weekends when I was working late, he would just go on over to the apartment. Peter would let him in, and he would wait for me to get off of work. I was still bringing him the French vanilla Hot Fudge sundaes. Tyler and I were really close. My boyfriend had become my best friend.

Peter and I were working out well as roommates. He had always been such a kind, sweet and supportive brother. We always paid our mutual expenses on time. We ate all of the same foods. This made grocery shopping uncomplicated. We were both thin, so neither of us had to avoid eating anything that the other one bought. When I was young, I was allergic to several foods such as eggs, oranges, and chocolate, but I had outgrown those thank goodness because these were now some of my favorite things to eat. I was neater than he was, but he could do what he wanted with his bedroom and bath as long as our shared living space was kept tidy and clean. Besides, he really didn't ever spend time in the living room watching TV or anything. He and one of his friends from his class at the technical college, frequently did their homework and studying at the dining room table. Even so, when I saw them there, I was usually only passing through the living room on my way out of the door, headed to class or work.

After a while, things began to change. Peter started acting differently. He was becoming argumentative. This was unusual behavior for my brother because he had always been pleasant, nice and reserved. I didn't quite know what to make of it. What I did know was that I did not like discovering this side of his personality. More often than not, I found myself calling Daddy in Birmingham, telling on Peter and asking our father to be the moderator. The arguments were happening much too frequently. On one occasion, he actually jerked the phone out of the wall because he became so upset when I reached for it, in an attempt to call Daddy. He even became so angry one time that he yelled at me and said Tyler could not come over here anymore. As far as I was concerned, this was all of the confirmation I needed, to feel that he had lost his mind! As if the fighting weren't enough, he started to become irresponsible by not providing his part of the rent and utility money when the bills were due. When I informed Daddy about this, he advised me to move out. He said, "Separate yourself from Peter because I suspect he is on drugs or something." He reiterated this to me a couple of times and said, "I don't want him to get so angry that he ends up hurting you."

My father was a very wise man. I valued his opinion and trusted his good advice. So, I proceeded by following the lease guidelines in order to ensure that my name was legally removed, and I informed my brother that I was moving out. Just as I anticipated, he became infuriated. He probably felt blindsided. However, it didn't matter. I had already made my decision. I could no longer trust him, and up until this bizarre behavior that Peter was now exhibiting, I trusted him completely with my life. Sadly, this was going to change my close relationship with my brother, and I didn't know if it would ever be able to be salvaged. In fact, I didn't even know what it would take to repair it. All I knew was that if he was on drugs, as Daddy was inclined to think, I could not condone this behavior because it went against my moral beliefs. I wasn't going to be able to overlook and ignore it.

This was my brother. He was supposed to be better than this. I was proud of him. He had already beat the odds. He was failing all of his classes in high school, so he quit and joined the Army. When he returned, all he wanted to do was go back to school. So, he did and excelled in his classes, which proved that all he needed was to have the desire to learn. He just did not have it when he was in high school. I did not understand why he was choosing to regress now. He had come so far. Finally, my life was nice, easy, and stable. Why did he have to go and cause this havoc? I had to pray for him and then leave it in God's hands because right now, I had to find a new place to live.

"Until you spread your wings, you'll have no idea how far you can fly."

Unknown

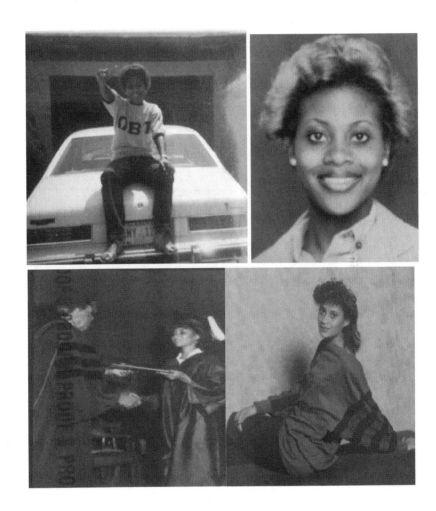

CHAPTER 5
On My Own

I remembered recently passing a sign that was advertising some new month to month rental studio apartments, just off of University Drive. I decided to call them because I needed to find a temporary place to live. I just wanted to be able to destress. I had to relax and get rid of all of the tension that I had been under. The Warren House studios sounded like a short-term answer, at least until I could come up with a more carefully thought out plan of action.

I decided to go ahead and rent the studio apartment until I found a more desirable place to call home. I felt like I was living in a hotel room because it was exactly the same size as one. The tiny bathroom (shower only), kitchenette and two single beds which I right away pushed together in order to make one large bed, were most certainly typical characteristics of one.

In spite of everything, living at The Warren House was just what I needed. I now had my own place where I could concentrate on my studies. It was also a real haven for me to come home to after a long day at school or a busy night at work. I felt like God was methodically teaching me how to become an independent adult really fast. It was like He wanted me to realize that in this existence, I could really only depend on Him and myself. This was a lesson that I would utilize over and over again during my lifetime. Even now, when I occasionally seem to forget and feel that others should be here for me, I am quickly reminded that He is the only one who will always be here for me. The wonder of it all is that He has never failed me, and I truly believe that He never will.

I was very relieved to be out of the unpleasant environment with Peter. Still in all, I could not help but be concerned for my brother. I wanted to be able to help him in some conceivable way. However, I did not know what I could do for him, mainly because I didn't know anything about drug addiction. Besides, I was only a 20-year old college student. What did I know about an Intervention? The

85

one thing I did know to do, was to pray for him daily. I asked God to protect my dear brother from harm, deliver him from this demon and to please always keep Peter very close. I also asked Him to keep knocking at the door of Peter's heart.

I lived there for about six months, then I was ready to move on. A couple of friends who were in my clothing and merchandising major were renting rooms from a young lady who took some classes at A&M. She had a house with six rooms on Blue Springs circle which included a downstairs den that could be used as a bedroom. All of the rooms were rented out, except for one. So, I moved in downstairs and had the largest room in the house for only 75 dollars a month. It wasn't the best-looking house, but it was surely full of smiling faces, laughter and some good times. The house was a split level, and my room was the spacious den on the bottom floor. The room had one window, but it didn't get much sunlight. It had built in bookshelves, which was a feature I did like. They added character and personality to my new living space.

Initially, there was a spider situation going on downstairs, and I don't know how I was able to sleep at night because I happen to have severe arachnophobia. Oh, I can remember entering the room after coming in from class or work and having to duck in order to keep from running head on into a web that I knew wasn't there that morning when I left out or even worse, staring into the eyes of one of the friendly eight-legged creatures as it was lowering itself down on a web. I had nightmares where I would open my eyes and see a huge monster spider hanging down over my head. The vision seemed so real that I would actually lunge out of bed from underneath it, trying to evade the horrific creature. This recurring bad dream continued even long after I moved out. The good thing was that I am a neat freak. So, I just kept my room immaculate and well-stocked with plenty of bug spray. I guess the spiders eventually decided to go back outside to live. Another disadvantage was that this house only had one bathroom, and it was upstairs. Imagine six women sharing one bathroom.

Our landlords were two young ladies who were best friends. Candice was overweight. She was caramel brown with long thick hair which she usually wore pulled back in a ponytail, and she had a pretty face. Lindsay had a dark brown complexion, and she wore a short layered haircut. She had a small shapely figure, and she only had one arm. When she went out in public, she wore an attachment inside of her sleeve that had a rubber hand on the end of it. I don't really remember if she was born without the limb or if she was an amputee. However, she was able to do everything she needed and wanted to do.

Candice and Lindsay were just about the only ones who used the kitchen. The rest of us usually brought fast food home for dinner. Now of course, if anyone was fortunate enough to have a microwave in their room, they kept some frozen foods in the freezer. Microwaves had become pretty common by the time I was 20 and 21. I didn't have one, so I was living off of fast food and Piccadilly's at the mall. Back then, they didn't have the stand-alone restaurants like now, where you can pull into the parking lot, and go right in and get your food. However, it wasn't too inconvenient because we only had four malls, and all of them were one-story shopping centers, so it was pretty easy to get in and out of the cafeteria quickly. There was a mall close by, and sometimes I would stop by and pick up dinner to go.

Every day Candice and Lindsay prepared home cooked Southern meals, like the ones your mothers and grandmothers made. On any given evening I could come home, and either Lindsay or Candice would be frying chicken, pork chops, pan fried steak or baking dinner in the oven. The other one would make macaroni and cheese, rice and gravy, mashed potatoes with real butter, collard or turnip greens, and cornbread. Sometimes, they even baked a cake to go along with their meal. They were always cooking something that filled the house with a wonderful aroma. Of course, the meals were not for any of the rest of us. The two of them bought their groceries together. Even with one arm, Lindsay would do just as much of the cooking and cleaning as Candice. In fact, she often did the dishes afterward. She carried things around by putting or hanging them on her shoulder. She washed, blow dried and somehow managed to curl her own hair. I remember Lindsay washing and folding her laundry. She ironed her own clothes. She even swept, mopped and vacuumed the floor. She performed all of these tasks using only one arm. Lindsay learned how to do almost everything for herself. Oh, she was an extremely independent young woman. I believed she could do just about anything she wanted to... except maybe drive, and she probably could have mastered that, if she desired to learn. However, I don't know if they would have given her a license.

It was God's plan for me to meet and become acquainted with this incredible young lady. He hoped that I would see Lindsay's strength, really take a good look at her and notice how positive she was about her life, despite her noticeable disability. It was almost as if He instructed me to pay close attention to her and the manner in which she accomplished things. He wanted me to remember her and this highly encouraging situation. She appreciated the gifts, talents and abilities which God gave her and never seemed to be pessimistic about anything, especially her physical challenges. She had an amazing will to be independent. She set high expectations for herself, managing to achieve and often exceed her goals one by one. I am certain, it was no coincidence that I was introduced to her. I learned so very much from Lindsay, more than anyone would ever know, including me. I had no idea she would make such an impact on my life.

I was taking English Literature, Human Anatomy and Voice and Diction (public Speaking). I had my work cut out for me. Human Anatomy and English Literature were two of my favorite subjects, so it would not be difficult to get an A or B in these two classes. I was looking forward to the Voice and Diction/Public Speaking course because I anticipated that by taking it, I would improve my self-assurance and assertiveness. These were two qualities that I wanted to transform.

I was really enjoying my Voice and Diction class, and my main purpose for enrolling in it was for the public speaking segment. All of my life I was terrified at even the thought of talking in front of a group of people. I felt like the only way to overcome this fear, would be to take a class. I saw the benefits from the very beginning of the course. All semester long, the instructor had been preparing our class for an important assignment. At the end of the course, we had to give a formal oral presentation. The audience was going to be an assembly of his combined classes. We were allowed to choose our subject, and if we failed to provide him with our selection by the deadline which was in about a week, he would assign a topic to us. I had no idea what I wanted to speak about and to be honest, I was very nervous just thinking about it. I decided that I would spend the weekend in the library searching for topics because the last thing I needed, was to be unprepared on the following Monday.

After examining books and reviewing newspaper articles and encyclopedias, I carefully investigated some topics by studying and analyzing anything and everything that I could get my hands on while I was in the library that weekend. I had never worked so hard on an educational project before and was still trying to decide on my subject. I narrowed my choices down to:

1. The Process of Child Adoption 2. The Human/Canine Bond

These subjects were and still are, very endearing to my soul. My brother Peter was adopted, and I really wanted to know everything about the methodology. As for my second choice, I have always been an avid animal lover. I still am. We always had dogs, and I was very intrigued by the unique relationship they have with humans. I was beginning to come to the realization that when one is passionate about something, the way I was about these subjects, you will look forward to communicating about it. So, what's to fear? Will it really matter that you are in front of a room full of people? I really didn't know yet, but I thought it sounded like a pretty good concept.

I decided to discuss The Process of Child Adoption. I wanted to be able to give what I learned to my brother. At least, in this case my theory did work because I did a really good job. I delivered a presentation which was very well planned and researched. I felt confident that I was assertive and articulate. I made sure to make good eye contact with the audience. I even gave them Q&A for a few minutes. I was almost sure that the added group interaction would help my overall grade. I was proud of myself for having the courage to fight this battle because I won. It was not easy being shy. Today, I am still a little nervous at the thought of public speaking. However, the difference is that I am confident, I can achieve it.

My relationship with Tyler was being challenged. In fact, we weren't doing so well. I was hearing rumors that he was involved with someone else on campus. Of course, this news more than bothered me, but first I needed to validate what I was told before I reacted. Once it was confirmed, and I'll admit, not without just a little bit of retaliation first and then some resistance, I remembered the saying...

If you love something, set it free; if it comes back, it's yours. If it doesn't, it never was. ~Richard Bach

Prior to this, where Tyler was concerned, I was not sharing, and believe it or not, as small as I was... I would not hesitate to confront any young lady who wanted me to even consider it! I saw her once in an auditorium. I wasn't intimidated at all by her appearance. I thought of her as simple. She didn't seem like his type. I approached her and introduced myself. I also let her know that I was Tyler's girlfriend. She had no words for me, and I had nothing more to say to her. I stated my case, then I simply turned and walked away.

With that being said, Tyler was away from Huntsville on a Cooperative Education program (better known as a Co-op) for his engineering major, when I started my college internship. I was going to be working in a department store named Parisian. Parisian was a chain of large high-end department stores both established and operated in Birmingham, Alabama. During the 1980s, they were in competition with Nieman Marcus, Nordstrom, and Gus Mayer. Saks took over in 1998, and in 2006, Belk purchased the stores. There were a few stores in Michigan, performing under the name of Parisian until 2013. I was with Parisian for seven years of my young adult life, so even though I was no longer with the company, I experienced a little nostalgia when they went through the restructurings, mergers, and acquisitions.

One day while I was working in handbags and accessories, one of my friends and co-workers who was also in my clothing major, asked me if she could introduce me to one of her male friends who worked at Bills London Transit (a men's clothing store) which was there in the mall. I didn't see any harm in meeting him. Besides, I was so picky that I probably wouldn't like him, and even though I didn't want to have feelings, I still cared about Tyler.

On our break, we took a walk down the mall corridor to the store where he worked. London Transit was on a corner. It was a large, open, modern store with quite exotic fixtures and silver metallic mannequins. The store had two levels and a metal winding staircase. Popular rock, pop, and R&B music could be heard over the intercom. The apparel was for the younger, stylish man.

As soon as we entered the store they saw each other, and he immediately walked over and met us with a nice friendly smile. Instantly, I recognized him. First, they greeted each other, then his hazel eyes focused on me. Alecia introduced us. She looked at me with a smile and said, "Shirley, this is Alton." Then she looked back at him and said, "Alton, this is my friend, Shirley." We exchanged hellos and had some casual conversation. I thought to myself, he doesn't realize it, but we have seen each other before. However, I would tell him about it later. Alton invited us to go out for a bite to eat after work. Alecia said she couldn't but encouraged me to go with him. I did want to go, so I accepted. We only had a few minutes left on our break, so we left and headed back to Parisian. This was before cell phones, so he didn't ask me for my number yet. He said he would meet me in the parking lot behind my store, shortly after nine PM. He was really nice, and I was looking forward to getting to know him better. I was very enthusiastic about our date after work.

To say the least, the feeling was undoubtedly mutual. We had a lovely evening. We spent it talking, laughing and getting to know one another while eating Pepperoni Pizza and enjoying a glass of Cabernet at Terry's Oven. I know it sounds cliché, but Alton was a breath of fresh air.

As the days and weeks went by, Alton and I spent quite a bit of time together. I met his family and often visited their home. He was a year younger than I was, and he and his younger sister lived at home with their parent's. There were six of them altogether. The others were older and had their own families. We would spend time with them at their homes on the weekends, eating very good food (because each of his sisters loved to cook) and playing cards or popular word guessing and party games. We watched the music videos which were new and popular, and it was my first time seeing Whitney Houston's. I remember playing with their kids and just having a really good time. I loved being around his relatives. They were the epitome of an extremely close family who loved each other unconditionally. I believe if you are blessed to have this, you are rich. The significance of family is that they give the kind of love that has no boundaries. You have a network of loved ones who truly care about you and your well-being, and they are your support system. Oh, and coincidently, I learned that our fathers knew each other. In fact, they played pool together in the past.

I was pressing my fingertips together and shaking my hands out because I was feeling tingling sensations. It was as if my fingertips were going to sleep. It wasn't the first time this occurred nor would it be the last. Anyhow, it ceased after a while, then I wouldn't think about it anymore. At least, not until the next time it happened. You see, there always seemed to be a next time, so I assumed it was normal. It was an infrequent occurrence, yet it seemed somewhat ordinary to me. I even asked Alton if he ever experienced this feeling before, but he said he wasn't familiar with it. Strangely enough, it was something that continued to happen over the next few decades.

I realized that I needed a part time job in order to supplement my income. I decided to get a job as a waitress at a local pizza establishment. To be able to still spend time with each other, Alton and his friends would often dine in. He had a good friend from Birmingham named Kaga who he brought in occasionally. Kaga was to put it mildly, intriguing and quite interesting to be around. He had an alternative lifestyle, but he seemed like good people. So, when Alton explained their friendship to me and I got to know him much better, I was totally comfortable with Kaga being in our company... at least, for some of the times. Alton had done some modeling, and he had a diverse set of friends. He had a charismatic personality, and he was very sociable. Everyone was drawn to him and wanted to be one of his friends. Have I mentioned that he just happened to be gorgeous? You can only imagine how pleasantly surprised I was when Alecia introduced me to him, and I finally got to know... that beautiful boy who came into Baskin Robbins that day with Maureen, back when I was in high school.

Every waitress or waiter that I have ever seen carries in a tray with several drink orders on it, and it's usually held with one arm up over their head. Of course, that was not something I was able to do. I did not think about that at all when I applied for the job. In fact, I don't think the shortcoming even crossed my mind when I carried the drink orders into the dining room on a tray with both arms held straight out in front of me. I didn't have the balance to do it any other way. I wasn't cut out to be a waitress. That's why I only kept the job for a couple of more months. I gave my notice and let it go at the end of the summer.

After deferring it for a couple of years, Alton had finally made up his mind to start college. He no longer wanted to put if off and watch others getting ahead of him. Those were his words not mine, but honestly, it had been a while since he had graduated from high school. The last thing I wanted was for him to attend school out of state. However, I was supportive because he was showing some interest in furthering his education by developing a career in something other than retail. I felt that both of us should not be working in retail because obviously, if we were going to ultimately be together and have any kind of a solid financial future, one of us should have ambition in a more lucrative career. Besides, I did not know what career opportunities my merchandising degree would present.

He and his parents finally decided on attending a University in Nashville, Tennessee. The first things I wanted to know about were how much distance was going to be between us and how long it would take for us to get to one another, then I would let him tell me all about what he wanted to study and everything else. Although, I wanted this change for him and was definitely one of his biggest cheerleaders, it was difficult when the time came for him to go.

It was a seemingly everlasting semester. Alton wasn't returning home very often, the way I anticipated he would. I didn't expect him to want to remain in Tennessee on the weekends. It was only 116 miles from Huntsville. He was 1 hour and 52 minutes away from me. I didn't understand, and I couldn't make sense of any of it. It seemed as if everything between us was okay when we talked every day on the telephone. Remember, there were no cell phones. So, communication was limited to talking on the dorm lobby phones or an off campus pay phone booth, if you were desperate or in a situation that appeared to be hopeless, such as a long wait at the lobby phone. Things just weren't the same. Alton was distant and not at all like himself anymore. I couldn't help but wonder if this was the beginning of the end.

One night while on the phone, we made plans for me to come to Nashville for the weekend. I was going to leave for Nashville on Friday after work and return home to Huntsville on Sunday. Alton changed the plans without having a conversation with me. Someone at the service desk at Parisian handed a piece of paper to me as I

94

passed by. It was a phone message from Alton. It stated that he was going to be studying all weekend for an exam, so do not come to Nashville, after all. I couldn't imagine why he changed his mind. However, I was determined to find out in person. Needless to say, I made the drive anyway. As a matter of fact, I made it there in 1 hour and 30 minutes.

When I called the phone in his hallway, someone was able to get him to come to it. He came out of the dorm and took me and my things back inside while asking me, "Didn't you get my message"? There were three or four guys just sitting around in his room, and one was playing a guitar. Alton introduced me to them, then they excused themselves... all of them, except for one. One guy seemed hesitant at first, but seconds later, he left also. Alton was acting out of the ordinary. I didn't recognize him. This guy who fell so much in love with me over the summer, did not seem to want me there. I was hurt. However, he wouldn't or maybe he just couldn't, say anything to make me feel better. He asked me if I was tired, but before I answered, he told me to get some sleep because I had to leave and go back home in the morning. He reiterated that he had to study that weekend for an exam. He knew I was aware of this already, even though I acted like I wasn't. He was distant that night and didn't have much to say.

The next morning, when he walked me to my silver hatchback Mustang and put my bag in the car, I knew that it was over between us. He didn't have to say anything, and we never discussed it, but I knew it was final.

My Mustang finally crossed over the Alabama state line. It really didn't take long. I was back in Huntsville before I knew it. I had a lot to pre-occupy my mind during the lonely ride home. I decided to drive straight over to Ridgewind Apartments on Sparkman Drive and visit Tyler. I knew he was capable of lifting my spirits, and right now, well they were at an all-time low. Understandably, I was just blindsided. The fact that he was the one and only person who I even thought of for comfort and support, confirmed in my heart that he really was my best friend.

As I turned onto his street, I was still rehearsing in my mind, exactly what I wanted to say about what just happened. There were about eight newly built, brick apartment buildings, and each one housed eight units. Tyler's was on the first-floor walk in level. I was no stranger over here. I had visited a few times before. Tyler knew that I was now with Alton. However, we were able to maintain an amicable relationship.

The element of surprise was written all over his face after I knocked on the door, and he quickly opened it and saw me standing on the other side. I walked into his apartment before he even invited me. It was brand new (still smelling of fresh paint and recently laid carpet) and furnished with only a waterbed, one of those saucer wicker chairs (which are now vintage), a 13-inch TV and a small wooden dinette set. All of a sudden, I began to tear up. That was a surprise even to me because I didn't want him to see me cry about Alton. Tyler was there for me during a time which would have been more difficult to face all by myself. I was so grateful for his friendship.

Obviously, Alton and I were shown to each other for a reason but only meant to be together for a season because I soon received a very short and sweet apology letter from him telling me that he couldn't handle the pressures of both school and a relationship.

Alecia and I made the decision to get an apartment and be roommates. We moved into Westwind Apartments, just off of Drake Avenue. Our apartment was on the second level. Tyler could dart up and down those steps without even holding on to the handrails. I didn't mind stairs, but I carefully walked them and definitely had to hold on. What he was able to do on the stairs was a skill, and I was amazed every time I saw someone perform it so well. I've always had a desire to be able to do it myself, but my mind and feet wouldn't even be able to figure out how. I couldn't help but wonder, why. I even asked him once, how to do it. He just laughed and said, "It's all in your balance and coordination." I thought to myself, you've got that right.

It was 1 1/2 bedrooms. I agreed to take the small room which had barely enough space for a full-size bed and a very small dresser. It was so small that it was almost funny. I had to exit my bed from the foot of the bed. It was exactly wall to wall, and I'm not exaggerating. I didn't mind though. I was just glad to have a friend for a roommate and someone who wanted to split the rent.

The Christmas holiday season is my favorite time of the year, and Santa was especially good to me for Christmas in 1983. Tyler surprised me with a ring. I wasn't expecting it. I had no idea. It was a small and simple solitaire. However, it was so beautiful to me. We called it our promise ring.

Our relationship wasn't perfect. However, we loved one another unconditionally. We had many conversations about the future, and the one thing we were sure about was that in it, we wanted to be together. I took Tyler to Birmingham with me a couple of times. Daddy was very protective, but he seemed to like him well enough. One Christmas, Tyler took presents that he bought for me, to Daddy and Lula's for safe hiding. I'm sure that set well with Daddy. So, I guess by then he approved of him. I met his parents in Gulf Shores, when I went home with him for Christmas one year. Once, we even took my sister Cynthia and her boyfriend from UNA, along with us to his parent's home for the holiday. They were really nice, and I got along well with his mother. She and I talked on the phone every now and then. Tyler and I were really good together, and we could see ourselves with each other for the rest of our lives.

I received a very large Manilla envelope in the mail. It came from Nashville, Tennessee. It was from Alton. The last time I saw him was about a year ago in Nashville. Inside of the envelope was an 8x10 black and white glossy photo of himself and a long-unfolded letter. In the letter, he said exactly what I wanted to hear him say that weekend when I was there but didn't. He told me that he still loved me, and he apologized for everything, including ending our relationship. He went on to say that he was quitting school because college was much more intense and overwhelming than he had anticipated. He was leaving Nashville and returning to Huntsville. He asked if I could find it in my heart to see him. I never replied to his letter.

It was not difficult at all to locate someone in Huntsville. With that being said, Alton called me and asked if we could have dinner and maybe see a movie. I was feeling torn. Ever since I received his letter, feelings which I had thought were buried, were resurfacing. It wasn't fair to give him an answer before discussing this with Tyler. Even so, I accepted. Of course, it didn't go over well when I told him that I was going to see Alton that evening. I didn't mean to cause this, but I could tell that Tyler felt insecure and threatened. These were two characteristics that I had not ever seen in his personality before.

Alton came back to Huntsville. Unsure about my unresolved feelings for him... honestly, I was looking forward to dinner. However, after spending that short amount of time with him, I was completely sure. My heart was with Tyler and only Tyler. Almost just as soon as I was back home and inside of my apartment, I heard a knock at the door. Surprisingly, it was Tyler. I let him in. He asked me how my date went, and I answered, "It was okay." He admitted to me that he was outside waiting for me to come home, and he watched us when I did. I didn't believe him. That wasn't his MO (method of operating). He told me that he saw everything, including Alton getting out of the car and taking a leak in the bushes. Then I knew he really was there.

The next time that I saw Alton was when he showed up at our apartment door over at Westwind one evening near Christmas. He looked like one of Santa's elves, standing there with a bag full of presents for me. I opened the door. However, I did not invite him in because Tyler was visiting. His smile went away when I sincerely thanked him for the gifts, told him I had company and that I would call him later. I gently closed the door while he was still standing there. I felt awful because he had gone to so much trouble. More importantly, I felt sad because I hurt his feelings.

Tyler actually graduated one semester before me. Frankly, I graduated a semester late. He accepted a position with a company in Atlanta, Georgia. It was his first job. You see, Tyler was spoiled as a child. He was his parent's favorite and the only one of their children to attend college. For that reason, except for the Co-op, he never needed to have a job before. Only, this was not just a job. This position was the beginning of his career.

I guess I didn't do very well with executing my good study habits during my final semester because I was failing Philosophy. I had a consultation with my instructor, and he assured me that he would not accept any make-up work from me in order to improve my grade. He firmly advised me that my final exam would ultimately determine my overall grade average. I really buckled down and committed all of my spare time to studying.

It was only two weeks before graduation, when the academic advisor in my clothing and merchandising major notified me that one of my instructors turned in a failing grade for me. However, it was rectified because it was determined that Philosophy was not a required course under the new curriculum, after all. I immediately said a prayer to my God, thanking Him for His unlimited grace and oh so sweet mercy.

Graduation Day was finally here, and I was so thankful to God for bringing me to it. I had not spoken to Daddy and Lula that morning. However, I previously informed them of the time and other details and felt confident that they were on their way. They were not making a weekend event out of it (that just wasn't how they rolled), even though some of the students had family who had been in "The Rocket City" for not only the weekend but the entire week. Nevertheless, I was going to be proud and happy to see them, even if only for the day. I don't remember the reasons why my brother and sister weren't at the academic exercise which was a celebration of this important milestone. Tyler wasn't there either, but it was okay because I was "Walking on air." When I accepted my diploma and walked across the stage, that Philosophy Professor was sitting up there along with the others, and I made sure to look straight into his bifocals... giving him the best eye-contact ever!

When the graduation was over, I saw Daddy. He had a polaroid camera around his neck. It was the kind where you take a picture, it slides out and then you watch it develop right before your own eyes in about five minutes. The thing was that I never saw any pictures. Lula wasn't with him. He said he dropped her off at her girlfriend's house so they could have a visit. I couldn't help but wonder if Daddy arrived late and didn't even see me walk and receive my honored recognition of achievement. Previously, he said that they would take me out to my restaurant of choice. I wanted a steak dinner. I'd never had a steak dinner before. Everyone had steak before prom, but remember, I didn't attend mine. So, we went to get Lula, but while we were there, her girlfriend invited us to eat squash casserole for lunch. She said she just baked it. I could hardly believe it when they said, "okay," and we sat down to eat. Obviously, I didn't get to have my steak dinner. I was very disappointed, to say the least.

Now that the commencement exercises had taken place, it was time for me to pursue my career interest with Parisian. I had a meeting one morning with Mr. Timmons, the personnel manager. He was my department manager when I did my internship in accessories. He had recently been promoted to this hiring position. I expressed my interest in the career opportunities with the store. I was surprised and extremely disappointed when he responded by saying that he didn't feel I had management qualities because I was quiet. He said I needed to be more outspoken in order to be a leader authority over other employees. Therefore, he did not feel that I was ready for the management program yet.

I was determined to prove him and anyone else for that matter who perceived me as too quiet to achieve any goal which I desired... wrong. I decided to apply for the Black cosmetic counter manager position that had just become available because Louise-the previous REP, recently transferred to the Madison Square Mall. We called it,

"The new mall." It was a two-story supermall that had recently opened its doors in the nearby City of Madison. I felt very confident that I helped to increase the small customer base and exceeded the previous sales representative's revenue. So, I believed that I helped enable the store location to continue to carry the product line. I proved to myself that I was indeed an incredible asset to the store's cosmetic department, and the best part was that with my pay plus bonuses, my income was about the same as what I would have made as an assistant department manager but with less stress.

Parisian was opening up a new location in the brand-new Riverchase Galleria Mall in Birmingham, Alabama. I decided that I wanted to transfer. My plan was to live there for one year, get used to driving on major highways (because back then Huntsville only had two overpasses), then permanently relocate to Atlanta, Georgia. I was almost ready to join my Tyler in the ATL, but I wanted to do this first.

My new sales position in Birmingham was a designer fragrance counter manager. So, not only did I leave the Huntsville store, I left the cosmetic line, along with Mr. Timmons. In any case, by making this change, I was sure to increase my income by several thousand dollars because the product was much more expensive. I liked living in Birmingham. "The Galleria," as we locals referred to it, was a deluxe upper-class super shopping mall with over 200 stores. It opened on Feb 28th, 1986. It was close to Birmingham. I had so much fun and some of the best times in my life while l was there. My co-workers became my new friends and associates. Our store and our mall was absolutely beautiful.

Even though my dad and Lula were in the same city, we hardly ever saw each other. I felt that Daddy was judgemental. Therefore, I think we both agreed that our lives would go much easier if we lived them as separately as possible, but there was an exception. There was an instance when Tyler was visiting from Atlanta. Daddy just happened to come over early one morning totally unannounced because he was doing some business at the bank which happened to be in the area. It was about 8:00 in the morning. I didn't answer the door because I must have been in the shower and didn't hear the knocking. I had to be at work by 9:30. When I pulled out of my parking space, he quickly pulled up behind me. He got out of his car and began questioning me about why I didn't answer the door and who was in my apartment. Of course, I said, "No one." Telling him the truth would have resulted in either his having a heart attack or him putting me into an early grave. Then he insisted that I open the door to my apartment so he could go in and see for himself. When I didn't comply, he demanded. I responded by telling him that I would not because I was an adult. Needless to say, my unwillingness to obey, resulted in Daddy leaving very angry at me and me being totally embarrassed and humiliated. In fact, we did not speak to each other for a couple of months. I wouldn't have been surprised if he sat out there and waited for someone to come out of my door after I left. I truly resented him for treating me like I was a child, and he was extremely disappointed in me, to say the least. For the first time in my life, I felt like I was really and totally, on my own.

"I like being a strong independent woman, and to be honest, I was never afraid to be on my own."

Dido Armstrong

CHAPTER 6
Georgia On My Mind

I had a plan for myself. I wanted to reside in Birmingham for one year, then I would move to Atlanta. I was visiting Tyler frequently in Atlanta. I went there at least two and sometimes three times a month. It was highly unlikely that I could have more than one weekend off in a month. So, usually I was there during the week. My department manager worked with me by letting me take both of my off days together so that I could stay for two days. Of course, Tyler still had to work, but I would be there when he came home. I would cook and surprise him with his favorite meals. He seemed to enjoy taking the leftovers for lunch the next day, so I always made extra. I was a pretty good cook, and I loved the way he let me practice new recipes on him. We dined out a lot, as well. There was always some new restaurant that he wanted to show me. One of his favorite things was introducing me to new dining experiences. Remember, we had already declared ourselves as "Eating buddies." Atlanta had so many places to eat. He was taking me somewhere new every week. I could not believe all of the shopping, and there were so many supermalls. We chose a different one for each shopping experience. My favorite was Lenox Square.

The first time I went to Atlanta was when I was a child. Daddy and Mrs. Blackwell took us to visit her sister, brother-in-law and their family. The next time, was with my high school Senior Class. We went to Six Flags over Georgia right before our graduation in 1979. Coincidentally, after we arrived we found out that one of the most popular groups of the great Disco Era just happened to be performing that night. Chic put on the best show ever, performing their hits "Good Times" and "I Want Your Love." They were my most favorite group of that genre. Needless to say, that trip was one of the best experiences of my youth.

All I could say was that Atlanta was amazing! Interstate 285 or I-285 was the interstate highway which encircled the city and was known as The Perimeter. It was both exciting and intimidating to me at the same time. However, Tyler did all of the driving, so I could just sit back and enjoy the ride, each and every time I visited. I loved it when we went for drives at night because there were lights everywhere. They were coming off of the buildings, restaurants, hotels and possibly bars and night clubs which appeared to be up on stilts, overlooking some parts of the Interstate. Even from a distance, the establishments were so inviting. It was as if they were competing with one another... each offering a more fun, exciting and enjoyable experience than the other. I would imagine what it was like to be on the inside of one of the far away venues. I'm sure people were talking and laughing. No doubt they were eating, drinking and some were probably even dancing. Whatever their pleasure, from my distant view behind the tinted windows of Tyler's black foreign sports car, I could tell that Atlantans really knew how to enjoy being out in their city at night, and we weren't even downtown yet.

My zodiac sign is Virgo, and to say the least, the definition of the sign is pretty typical of my personality. Some of the things that Virgos like are animals, books, and cleanliness (True). Some of the weaknesses are shyness, worrying and being extremely critical of themselves and others (Definitely). Virgo is a totally independent sign. We almost always work out how to get things done, using our intelligence (I do this so very often). We are also, notably analytical (Exactly). Virgos may choose a career as a writer or a journalist (Absolutely). Virgo's desire is to give love and have it reciprocated (Amen).

Tyler more than exceeded my expectations when we celebrated my birthday in the fall of 1984. I came to the city to spend a couple of days with him. On my special day, he surprised me with tickets to see one of my favorite R&B duos. Ashford and Simpson were performing at Atlanta's Chastain amphitheater. As if that weren't enough, earlier we had dinner at Dailey's. It was a nice landmark restaurant in downtown Atlanta. I had the Cornish Hen, and we both ordered Fried Ice Cream for dessert. It was the first time I had tried either one of them. I made good choices because I ate just about every bit of it. I don't know if it was living in a city which offered so many different forms of entertainment or the fact that he now had a lucrative income, but something definitely influenced Tyler to become interested in most everything the City of Atlanta had to offer. Nonetheless, I was definitely enjoying receiving the benefits of being his girlfriend.

The Temptation's hit "Treat Her Like a Lady," Wham's (featuring George Michael) song "Careless Whisper" and Sade's "Smooth Operator" were my favorite tracks during that time. They are so reminiscent of that period of my life. Whenever I visited, Tyler was very enthusiastic about planning our activities. We spent so much of our time on the phone talking about where he wanted to take me next. I saw this really thoughtful side of him, and it was so sweet. We did the horse drawn carriage tour which was in the heart of downtown Atlanta, and I will never forget the experience of the Sun Dial rotating restaurant & cocktail lounge at the top of the Westin Peachtree Plaza Hotel. We even managed to get away and go to Panama City Beach a couple of times when I was able to take off for a much-needed vacation from work in retail. We grew so close. We talked about marriage and spending the rest of our lives together. We even picked out a name for our first baby boy. We decided on the name Jonathon (a variant of Jonathan, which is of the origin, Yonatan).

I gave myself one year to be in Birmingham, and that year was coming to an end. Strangely enough, it actually almost seemed to be happening too soon. It's true what they say about time flying when you are having fun. I enjoyed working for this company. Except, for the minor injury to my self-esteem which was received from the feedback given to me by the personnel manager in the Huntsville store, this company had been very good to me. By relocating to Birmingham, acquiring the designer fragrance line and utilizing my personality, sales and good customer service skills, I was able to increase my income by 7000 dollars. No one was prouder of me than I was of myself. After all, I was a 24-year-old single female who was totally independent. I figured out how to make ends meet when you don't quite have enough. I learned this directly from my father. He was the wisest man I knew. I am so grateful to him for being both the momma and the daddy bird who pushed me out of the nest so that I could fly on my own... and I soared. Daddy gave me some really good advice once. He told me to be assertive, and always speak up. He said don't ever let anyone think that you are timid, or they might think that you are passive and lacking confidence.

I remember having a crush on my middle school band director. I was so very nervous around him that I would hyperventilate. I can remember him being up on the podium at the front of the band. He was simply talking to us, and I was sitting approximately 10 to 15 feet out from him with the French horns, yet I was having difficulty breathing. I was taking in all of this extra oxygen. Go figure. I would go through this for the first 15 to 20 minutes of the band period almost every single day. One day he and I were in his office for a consultation or a practice session or something. We were sitting only about three feet apart, and he could probably see my heart jumping out of my chest. I'm sure he noticed I was breathing so rapidly that I was quickly losing all of my carbon dioxide! Suddenly, he asked me, "Are you afraid of me"? I wanted to say, "No... I'm in love with you."

I kept a list of my personal achievements in my head in order to remind myself of how capable and tenacious I really was because sometimes, especially now... I tend to forget.

I bought my first car, a Chevelle Malibu, for 275 dollars cash when I was 18 and drove it for 2 1/2 years until I traded it.

I had my second vehicle financed. It was a used hatchback Ford Mustang. My car payment was 171 dollars, and I was only a junior in college.

I was a full-time college student who lived off campus and paid rent, utilities, car payment, food, etc., as any working adult would.

I obtained a bachelor's degree while maintaining two part-time jobs.

I relocated to another city at age 24 and lived totally on my own. My apartment rent was 285 dollars, and my second financed vehicle was a Pontiac. My car payment was 235 dollars.

Except, for the fact that my father sent me 40 dollars for an accounting book one time, I had absolutely no parental financial support whatsoever while I was in college nor did I have any assistance from them afterward. I still don't know how I did it. My daddy once told me that when I was a baby, he nicknamed me "The Survivor" because I was my mother's first full term pregnancy. He said that out of his three children, I was the one he never worried about. It was because I reminded him of himself. I was thinking the same thing. I reminded myself of him, likewise. I knew that my valued qualities of strength, independence and survival, all came from my father.

I enjoyed cooking full meals, even though I was the only one eating them, and I did not mind taking the leftovers for lunch. I was home preparing my dinner one evening when my sister called. Immediately, I heard the sadness in her voice. She told me that she had something very disturbing to talk to me about. I went to the stove and turned down the heat. I didn't want to forget about the food that was simmering, if I should become distracted. She began to talk to me about our brother. Evidently, he was going through some problems. She said he came over often, and she was lending a sympathetic ear. Recently, they had lunch at KFC, a popular fried chicken fast food restaurant. He confided in her about something very sensitive and quite devastating. She paused... I was listening but heard nothing but silence. She then said, "Shirley, Peter tested positive for HIV." I was at a loss for words. I wanted to do something to help him, but I had no idea what would. Peter and I had not made amends. I loved my brother, so I lifted him up in prayer every single day.

The date to give my two-week notice was soon approaching. I

was thinking nostalgically. After all, I practically grew up at this company, and I was going to miss the friends that I made. For the first time since high school, I would be unemployed. They had not yet opened any of our stores in the Atlanta Metro area. It would have made the transition so much easier if the chain had a location there. However, it would be a few years before Parisian came to the State of Georgia. I wasn't concerned though because I had ambition. I was excited about starting my brand-new life. I still had an interest in a retail management career, and Atlanta was going to be just the perfect city for me to make my dreams come true.

I wasn't the only clothing and merchandising major from my class at A&M to transplant themselves in the City of Atlanta with big aspirations. Alecia and Brandi (another graduate from our major) were already there. Alecia told me that Brandi was looking for a roommate because hers had recently moved out. This was going to work out perfectly because we were already acquainted with each other, and she was a really nice person.

If we traveled on I-20, Atlanta was exactly 146.5 miles away from Birmingham. That was only going to be 2 hours and 21 minutes. Besides, I was just a phone call away.

My car was already in Atlanta. I drove it there a couple of days ago and left it with Tyler. He brought me back so I could ride in the van with my daddy who affectionately called me his "First born."

The only furniture I was taking with me was my simple wood box framed waterbed, my 13-inch television (which I rented for eight months, so I now owned it) and a wicker table and chair. Daddy loaded it all into his church van, along with my clothes and other belongings, then we were on our way to Georgia. I was only 26 years old. However, I had wisdom, some bravery and quite a bit of good common sense. Besides, the world wasn't as crazy as it is now.

I'll always cherish the conversation between me and Daddy during the ride from Alabama because it was quality time spent together. He gave me some direct, immeasurable advice about life in general and experiencing this world as an adult. I was about to venture on an incredible journey. It meant the world to me that my father was taking me. I felt as if he was setting his dove free. It showed me that he trusted me with the lessons that he taught me. More importantly, he felt that I was mature and responsible enough to face whatever challenges might occur. Although, I did not need his approval, he was giving me his total validation. He hoped that I would always remember my Christian values... to read my bible daily and never forget the most important thing, which is prayer.

Daddy followed the directions to get to Smyrna without any difficulty, then I began to read them aloud in order to ensure that we didn't miss the exit for Cobb Parkway. "It says to turn left, right here Daddy, at the Clock Tower," I said. We were now here, and we arrived safely. With our eyes closed and our heads bowed, Daddy said a nice quick prayer, thanking God for His traveling mercy.

The apartments were a gated community. So, we called her unit, and she opened the tall iron gate remotely. The grounds were so beautifully landscaped. There were many trees, shrubs and flowers. They were everywhere. I was so sure that this detail impressed Daddy. The apartment complex was very attractive and extremely well kept. It had two and three-story buildings. I was excited about living there, and I could tell that the ambiance of my soon to be residence was beginning to ease Daddy's mind. I could not have asked God for a better welcome to my new home.

It was a second-floor apartment. We would have to get someone to help Daddy bring the waterbed frame and the wicker furniture upstairs. Brandi answered the door almost within seconds after we knocked. I guess she was just as excited to greet her new roommate as Daddy and I were to see mine. Knowing my father, he was very anxious to put a face to her name because before now, she had been fictitious. She was about to become a reality to him.

The apartment was really nice. There was no furniture in the living room. It was a large room full of seemingly new, light gray carpet. The kitchen was small but cute. It had an opening so that you could see into it without actually going in and a snack bar directly underneath it. There was a lengthy hallway and two large bedrooms, one with an adjoining bath and mine was in the hallway. We were able to get Brandi's neighbor to help Daddy bring the furniture upstairs. We filled up the waterbed, and once Daddy saw that I was situated, he left for Birmingham. I wanted to let Tyler know that I was here and all moved in as soon as possible. He would be home from work in a couple of hours.

The next few days were spent searching for a job. With a pen in one hand and a highlighter in the other, I must have looked through four newspapers before I finally saw it... an advertisement for an assistant manager trainee at a well-known store which specialized in dressing the career woman. The company was opening a petite's division. This sounded like the perfect position for me. After all, I did fit the bill. I was obviously petite and also, a career woman. As if that weren't enough. The location of the store was the "At Around Lenox" shopping plaza which was next door to Lenox Square Mall. This just happened to be my favorite mall in the Atlanta Metro area.

The entire process from application to interviewing took a couple of weeks. Meanwhile, so I would have some incoming funds for my food and gas, etc., I registered at a temporary employment agency. They sent me on several retail job assignments. Each one was part time hours and for one day only. These earnings were such a blessing.

Finally, I received a call from the personnel manager at the retail store, for the position which I had applied. They wanted to interview me. I was so excited. The management position that I hoped and prayed for was getting closer to being realized. I just had to practice patience and keep believing. I was really learning that perseverance does bring positive results. Of course, that call was just for the interview. However, now that I had the interview, I was sure to impress them, and get the job.

I wanted to share my news and excitement with the one who was always in my corner. So, I called Tyler. It was around noon on Saturday. I asked him if I could come over and he said, "Okay, sure."

Only, when I arrived and came up the steps to his second-floor apartment, a familiar female was standing in front of his door. It was the girl from A&M. When we were in college, I began hearing rumors of their involvement. She was the one. When I lived in Birmingham, Tyler mentioned to me that she moved to Atlanta, but he gave me his word that he only saw her once. He said he ran into her while she was working at the mall which was near his apartment in Smyrna. So, why was she here now, and how did she know where he lived? Why was she in front of his door? I was asking myself these questions, as if I had the answers. However, I was about to get them from both her and Tyler.

As I approached her I asked, "Does he know that you are out here, and why won't he open the door"? I already knew the answer to those questions. He was expecting me, but evidently, she showed up first. He wouldn't open the door, even when I announced that I was out there. He let us both just stand there looking stupid. I told her that I lived here now, then I said something mean and harsh. I honestly do not remember what it was that I said. However, I would never forget what she said in response. She said, "Did he tell you that I was carrying his child"?

I was stunned, knocked back. It felt like her words punched me directly in the stomach. Once again, I was blindsided. I decided to be nice to her. I apologized. All I could think about was that Tyler was a liar and a coward. This is why he would not open the door. I knew he was not going to come out here and face us. I left and went home feeling humiliated. Initially, I cried. Understandably, I was angry. I couldn't comprehend why he would let me uproot my life and move here when all of this was going on. Why didn't he tell me before I left my job... before I left Birmingham? What on earth did he think would happen once I became aware of this injurious and damaging situation?

I woke up this morning feeling extremely positive. I was more than confident that I would win over the owners (a husband and wife), store manager and hiring personnel, in my interview. If I were successful, I would train as an assistant manager and be next in line for the position in their newest store. The last several days had been intensely difficult for me, emotionally speaking. However, the most important thing to me right then, was getting an offer for this new position. I prepared myself. I rehearsed it. I was about to go in here and convince these important people who at the moment, were in complete control of my future (at least within their organization), that everything in my life was absolutely wonderful, and I was more than ready for this challenging position of authority in one of their stores. My goal was to leave them with the impression that I was the perfect candidate for this occupation.

Two lengthy weeks went by without hearing a word from Tyler. I couldn't help but wonder if it was because he was in contact with her. I should not have cared nor wanted to hear from him, but for some reason, I did. I think I just didn't want everything that we once were, to be a lie. It was strange, even to myself, but I missed him. Don't get me wrong. I didn't miss the guy who cheated on me. I missed my best friend. For months, we planned this. Just a few weeks ago, I moved here so we could be together, yet I was already all by myself. I wasn't even able to tell him about the management position. Did I mention it? I got the job at "Petite's-n-Co."

I just had the rug pulled out from under me, and I wasn't falling apart. So, I would say that I was handling it pretty well. After about three weeks, one evening the phone rang, and Brandi told me it was Tyler. I wasn't ready to talk to him yet, so I didn't take the call. He made a couple of more attempts over the next several days, and when I finally spoke with him, he was very apologetic. He told me that because he gave her no hope for a future together, she moved to Roanoke, Virginia to live with her sister and have her baby. I corrected him and said, "Your baby." He went on to say, he'd been praying that I could somehow forgive him because he couldn't go through life without me. In all honesty, I wanted to be able to trust him again because I didn't want to have to be without him either. I just didn't know if I could. I told him that I already forgave him, and

I was now willing to try and see if this could possibly work out. We both knew that accepting and dealing with this difficult situation was going to be a real challenge for me. While at A&M, he finally told me that he had a daughter with the girl who never returned after their freshman year. That was easier to accept because that happened prior to my knowing him. However, this new baby was conceived in the present, while he was supposed to be in love with me.

I wasn't making as much as an assistant manager trainee as I did when I was a fragrance counter manager. In fact, I was making about 4000 dollars less, and after a while, it began to take its toll on me. I accepted the position with the anticipation that I would be able to advance within this company fairly quickly, therefore increasing my income. I did not know how much longer I could hold out while waiting for the company to open another petite's store. To make matters worse, they wanted me to only wear their store's apparel to work. This meant that I would have to start spending my limited income on clothes. This store was a boutique. It carried many designer name brands. The clothing was kind of expensive. Initially, I tried to comply with their wishes, but this mandatory rule quickly put me in an uncomfortable financial situation. I had obligations and a roommate to consider and being late on my bills was definitely not an option.

I was at the store for about six months when I received a good lead on a job in an entirely different field. The pay was hourly plus monthly bonuses. This was intriguing to me. I followed up on the lead. On my day off, I drove halfway around The Perimeter to get to their facility. I applied for the position. I was pleased when I was called back for a second interview. I was seated and waiting in a small office when in walked a very tall, dark-skinned, slightly overweight, Black man with a mustache and a scruffy beard. He had a very loud, boisterous voice, and he used quite a bit of jargon or Southern slang. He sat down and introduced himself. He explained that if I paid close attention while in training and listened well to my leaders and colleagues, I could make a lot of money. He added that they would train me on everything I needed to know. Finally, he went over the bonus structure. He told me that the position was mine if I wanted it. I was so impressed with the information about the potential earnings that I didn't even mind the commute half way around The Perimeter. So, I accepted his offer to become a debt collector for delinquent, Department of Education (DOE) Student Loans. Now I had to go and face my employers and resign from my less lucrative retail management position.

I wasn't the only clothing major from my class at A&M who did not end up with a career involving merchandising or design. Brandi was in automobile sales when we became roommates, and she was making good money. Today, Alecia has a very successful real estate career.

I received a phone call from a familiar voice one evening. It was the voice of my on-campus sophomore college roommate, Olivia. I wasn't sure how she located me. I didn't know that she even knew I was in Atlanta. Later, she told me that a mutual friend of ours had given her my contact information. Unexpectedly, she wanted to meet up with me. She was going to be in Atlanta soon. She told me that she wanted to relocate here, and she was going to seriously begin searching for a job. We met for lunch, and to my surprise, we had a lot to catch up on and talk about. It turned out to be a nice outing, after all.

I made the decision to move from the apartment in Smyrna because it was much more expensive than what I could comfortably afford. The months that I spent working for the petite store making less money, really did set me back financially. I needed to make a change. Although my indecisiveness did sever my relationship with Brandi... at the time, I felt it was best that I move out and find a more economical place to live.

When you can see the light at the end of a tunnel, you're okay. It's when you don't see the light that you are in trouble. I strongly believe in and have always lived by this thought. Moving out to minimize my expenses was that light for me. By taking this action and being disciplined, I would soon be able to breathe again. I knew she didn't right then, but I hoped that one day she might understand and be able to forgive me for causing her this inconvenience. Not enough time had passed because Daddy said when he called for me, he was told that I no longer lived there, and I had moved in with Tyler. You can only imagine how difficult it was for me to convince him that was not the situation.

Tyler had a friend whose ex-wife had a room for rent. She lived in an okay area, and it wasn't far from the expressway. Although, I wasn't crazy about the idea of living in an older place and sharing her kitchen, I would be able to save a lot on rent, and she did have two full baths. I was definitely considering it.

Coincidentally, Olivia called and said she was coming back to Atlanta for a second interview with one of the pharmaceutical companies. She felt pretty sure that she was going to be offered the position. Since I worked a mid-shift, we made plans to meet for a late dinner. She had good news to share. They did make an offer, and she accepted. She would be relocating next week.

When I shared my dilemma with her, she immediately said she wanted to be roommates. At first, I was very hesitant. We had a lengthy conversation about it and promised each other to always openly communicate so that we would not repeat the mistakes we made when we lived in the college dormitory. I remembered how she was back at A&M. She would hold onto less than positive thoughts in her head, never discussing them with me, then she would erupt as soon as I said something that triggered her explosive personality.

Putting that aside, Olivia was a nice person. Most importantly, she was a Christian who had good morals and values instilled within her. She came from a close, loving family. She was much like me when it came to being mature, independent and responsible. More than likely, she was going to be a good roommate. We were in agreement on finding an apartment that was in a nice location, in a well-kept community, had eye appeal and was very affordable. I said a prayer to God, asking Him for His guidance, protection, and discernment. I also asked for plenty of patience because I had a feeling... I was going to need it!

"The heart was made to be broken."
Oscar Wilde

CHAPTER 7
Something's Not Quite Right

After being responsible for a situation which I am quite sure made Brandi more than dislike me, I was hoping that this one would surely work out. Olivia and I found an apartment with a roommate floorplan in Doraville. I am a very forgiving person, and I try to see the good in everybody. So, it was either that or I was just a glutton for punishment. Be that as it may, I did and I still do believe in giving second chances. I have even been known to give third and fourth. However, in those cases, I usually live to regret it. So, here we go again... was the common expression that I thought about for this particular scenario, except hopefully without the drama this time. I prayed about it and hoped I wasn't asking God for too much.

These apartments weren't gated, but back then we didn't have all of the outrageous crime that we do now. So, that amenity wasn't thought of as a necessity, like it is today. I wouldn't dare live in an ungated apartment complex these days, especially living in the Atlanta Metropolitan area.

We signed a one-year lease agreement and for the most part, got along very well as roommates. We started walking, jogging and even running at the nearby track. This was a really good thing because we encouraged each other and became accountable to one another. Believe it or not, becoming running partners actually seemed to strengthen our friendship, and roommates do need to be genuine friends. The ironic thing is that sometimes after the run, we would drive down to Ponce de Leon and get Krispy Kreme original glazed doughnuts when the HOT NOW light was on. Go figure.

One Christmas day, I had a bad cold and didn't go to Daddy and Lula's house in Birmingham. In those days, there was nothing open on Christmas, except for the Waffle House. Olivia went home to Mississippi. When she came back, she brought a nice big bowl of chitterlings home with her and put them away in the freezer. I remembered them from when my mother used to cook them for my father. So, when she warmed them up and asked me if I wanted some, I politely declined. She insisted that I just try them. She said, her aunt's "Chitlins" were the best. So, I told her I would taste one bite. They were certainly different. Surprisingly enough, I liked them. Actually, with the hot sauce they were very good, but I won't eat them without the hot sauce. So, Olivia is responsible for introducing me to this Southern delicacy. Give me a bowl full of Chitlins covered with hot sauce, and I am in "Hog heaven."

Everything changed in one day. I was on the phone when a second call came in on call waiting. I took a message for Olivia and gave it to her as soon as I finished my call. She read it and became furious. She began yelling at me, saying that I should have ended my call and told her to pick up because it was her aunt calling long distance. She actually wanted to fight over this, and the girl attacked me in the hallway with her long fingernails. She wouldn't let go of my hair, and she was purposely trying to scratch my face. I couldn't believe that we were actually fighting. Somehow, we made it into my room... probably through my attempts to get away from her and get her off of me. We fell over onto my waterbed. I decided to use psychology on her, and I began to talk at her while she was still fighting me. She wouldn't let go. I said loudly, "We are 27 years old and fighting as if we are teenagers. You are crazy"! Suddenly, she snapped out of her seemingly deranged fit of rage and stopped. Immediately I said to her, "Either you move out, or I surely will." She told me that she wasn't going anywhere. So, when she turned and stormed out of my room, I slammed the door and began to think about a plan of action.

Next door to our apartments, a new apartment community was about to open. They were attractive and honestly, looked pretty expensive. Nevertheless, I was going to inquire about them because I was determined to get out of that negative situation. Talk about history repeating itself.

Actually, I was pleasantly surprised when I visited the apartment community next door because it was within my budget. They had two different one-bedroom floor plans. I chose the smaller one for the time being. However, before I could fully commit by putting a deposit down on it, I needed to ensure that I would be able to get my name off of the other lease.

I made a visit to the leasing office before I headed back to the apartment to inform my soon to be ex-roommate of my intentions. The leasing agent gave me the form which had to be signed off by Olivia. It stated that she was authorizing my name to be taken off of the lease. I didn't think she would be opposed to it, but because of this most recent episode, I was beginning to feel threatened by her character. Besides, I couldn't imagine why she would want me to continue being her roommate, when I no longer wanted to be.

When I approached her with the form, I was astonished because she simply took the paper, signed it and handed it back to me. Then she turned and walked away without saying a single word. I didn't know which emotion I wanted to feel first. I was totally surprised at her refrainment, so relieved that there was no rebuttal and just plain happy that this situation would soon be coming to an end. This went so much better than I expected it would. I was so grateful that I did not have to experience any of her wrath or drama. I sat down to be still for a few minutes and gave thanks to the Lord because the only way I could imagine her remaining calm, was if the Holy Spirit was there in that room with us.

I moved into my beautiful new place. It was a compact apartment on the walk-in level, but it was plenty of room for me. Finally, I was experiencing the best peace that I could ever have. I had peace of mind.

Tyler had moved to Dunwoody, and I was living in Doraville. Our commute to see each other was now greater. He noticed that I was becoming distant. It was difficult for me to get over his disloyalty. The fact that he created a child with someone caused a deep wound that just wouldn't heal. Furthermore, even when and if it did heal, there would be an ugly scar. Later, I learned that she had the baby. It was a boy, and she actually named him Jonathon. She didn't spell it Jonathan or even Johnathan. That was the deal breaker for me. That was the name we were going to name our first. Needless to say, this was an extremely stressful time for me, and there were so many times that I just cried about it.

Tyler knew that I lost all trust and faith in him. I knew that going forward, I would only put my trust and faith in God. As far as I was concerned, if there is no trust, there is no real relationship. Tyler's employer offered him a promotion. However, it was contingent on his agreeing to relocate to South Florida. He accepted the offer. Then he asked me to go with him. I listened to my common sense and told him no, I would not be following this time. I knew in my heart, my unwillingness to relocate with him, meant I was ending our relationship.

Even though the income was pretty good, after a year, I grew extremely tired of the hustle and bustle of hardcore collections. It was definitely different and very rewarding, to say the least. I'll never forget... whenever a large sum of money was recovered and posted, that same loud collections manager stood up from his seat and made a blaring announcement that a BIF or SIF (balance or settlement in full) came in, and he would shout out the responsible collector's name. All of the bells and whistles went off, meaning that the other collectors would start clapping and cheering. He sounded like a big bad wolf, but it was so great for our self-esteem. It might sound funny, but I did not miss the appealing career of fashion, and this collections position was far from being glamorous. Even though you wouldn't have known this by looking at any of the employees. I remember wearing pumps, dresses or skirts and pantsuits to work every day. The males wore suits or at the very least, dress shirts and ties, slacks and probably their best pair of designer shoes.

I decided to explore some of the employment possibilities in the telecommunications industry. I interviewed and accepted a position with one of the leading nationwide long-distance corporations. It was one of the best decisions I ever made because my career with this organization lasted for 24 years. The dress code in corporate

America during the mid-80s and the early 90s was definitely suits or shirts and ties for men and dresses and slacks for the women. We wore heels. I didn't even own a pair of flats, and we were required to wear pantyhose. It was very different from today's more common dress code of business casual.

I worked in a few different departments within this corporation, throughout my career in telecommunications. Thanks to my most recent collections experience, my first position was in Residential Receivables. I also worked in Business Customer Service, Video Conference Reservations, Video Technical Support and ultimately, Business Customer Service again but as a telecommuter. There was one commonality of all of the positions. It was computer data entry. Therefore, it wasn't very surprising when I started to experience hand and wrist discomfort. After an office visit to my primary care physician, I was diagnosed with carpal tunnel syndrome, which is also referred to as median NERVE compression. It's a very common condition. In fact, there are a few million cases diagnosed in the United States, every year.

A pinched nerve was causing some pain, numbness and tingling feelings in my hand and wrist. My physician prescribed a wrist brace for me to wear. In mild cases, the condition usually resolves itself on its own. However, in severe cases, cortisone injections and even surgery is sometimes required to correct the problem. In my case it ended as suddenly as it began. Actually, I didn't even wear the brace that often or for very long. For these reasons, I assumed that this diagnosis was accurate. It made sense. Typing was 100 percent of my job description. I had no reason to doubt it or suspect anything else. If I only knew then what I know now, about what was really going on with my nervous system! And those symptoms... well, they did re-occur.

"Everything Isn't Always What It Seems"
~Whisper

Almost every day, I would go on fast walks and runs at the track at an elementary school on the corner. It was the one good thing that resulted from my knowing Olivia. Running was becoming a habit. I often spent three to four hours at the track, especially on beautiful sunny days over the weekend. I usually meditated when I fast-power walked, while soaking up the sun's rays. I valued the time I spent at the track. It was really therapeutic for me, and I considered it to be quality "me" time. Speaking of Olivia, about six months after I moved out and into my very own place, I upgraded to the larger apartment. I was listed in the phonebook (we were still using landlines). So, she called and apologized for what happened and her behavior. She wanted me to know that I was the best roommate she ever had, and the one she had now was a nightmare. I laughed and accepted her apology graciously.

Daddy called one morning. He was in a very solemn mood. He revealed to me that Peter finally informed him of his HIV diagnosis. He probably delayed telling him because he didn't know how to approach Daddy with this sensitive information about himself. My siblings and I had each experienced Daddy's judgemental wrath before. So, I could only imagine the apprehension he was feeling, when trying to decide when and exactly how he was going to tell our father.

Against my sister's advice, my brother made the mistake of confiding in a superior at his job. As a result, he was terminated. I'm sure he didn't know how to react. He experienced this second devastation, when he had not yet recovered from the first. Peter had a nervous breakdown.

Daddy said he drove his car to Birmingham and asked if he could stay there with him and Lula. I'm sure he wanted his father's emotional support and protection, but Peter said that Daddy didn't think it was a good idea. Lula tells me, they already had a boarder. According to Peter, Daddy was emotionally unavailable and unable to offer him the unconditional love that he needed. Our father called and informed us of our brother's mental condition. Daddy checked him into a VA hospital in Tuscaloosa. Lula says that he visited him daily. Cynthia now lived in Atlanta, and she was a newlywed. She and her husband decided to go pick him up, bring him to Atlanta and help him get into a good support program. Daddy was very good when it came to providing for us, teaching us right from wrong and keeping us safe from harm or injury. However, he wasn't the best when it came to showing us unconditional love, except for the time when my sister decided to separate from her first marriage. Daddy drove out of state to pack up her things and bring his baby girl back to Alabama. I think maybe all three of us knew this, but we never held it against him. Instead, we just loved him in spite of it.

Over the next couple of years, Peter struggled with his addiction. He was in and out of rehabilitation. I would hear from him when he was in treatment. When he did not keep in touch, it was because he was using again. There were times when he would call, and I would pick him up and take him grocery shopping. If he was in rehab, I would go and visit on family day. When he became bedridden, I would go to his apartment and clean it for him on Fridays after work. He maintained close friendships with Ms. Baxter, Daddy's ex-friend from Huntsville and her family. Peter had an extremely kind nature. He was the most selfless person that I have ever known. Unfortunately, my brother did not have the same strong will that Cynthia and I had. Sadly, he was unable to get his life back on track. He was an Introvert, much quieter than me. Unfavorably, he was very impressionable.

Since he had nowhere else to go, I suppose Peter felt as if he had no other choice but to stay here. However, the City of Atlanta was definitely not a good area for him to live. This was a large fast place. I would imagine that there was a lot of drug activity just waiting for a very nice, quiet, naïve and unsuspecting young man who was honestly trying to shake an addiction.

I think back to when we were roommates. Peter used to say to me, "I wish I could find a girlfriend who was just like you and Cynthia." When he confided in our sister, he shared with her that his initial exposure to drugs happened when he was stationed in Germany. He was a terribly naive 17-year-old teenager who had just completed basic training. I wish his life had been different. Why couldn't he have made better grades, remained in school and looked harder for that girl who was just like us because she was out there?

Peter didn't try hard enough to get his life back. He succumbed to the vices and his HIV status quickly developed into AIDS. Life became much too difficult for him to want to continue fighting. He lost his will to live. He stopped going to the doctor and taking his meds. His condition declined rapidly, and my beloved brother died in 1992 at the young age of 33. However, before he passed away, my brother was able to finally see and feel what he longed for all of his life.

Our father came to Atlanta to visit him several times. When I told him that I was cleaning Peter's apartment, he wanted to come and help me one weekend. I remember the time he was about to stick his bare hand in the toilet. I stopped him just in time and told him to put gloves on. Once, he came here and we all took pictures outside. Cynthia's oldest son Kelvin was a toddler, and Brian was a baby. Daddy was a proud granddad. On another weekend, we spent time with Peter at Grady Hospital. I watched as Daddy gently caressed my brother's head. When Peter told us he was thirsty, I reached for his plastic cup of water with a straw. He turned his head away and said, "I want Daddy to give it to me." So, Daddy did. I witnessed something so beautiful between them that day. Daddy finally gave Peter his unconditional love.

The next day, I brought my sister, so that they could say their goodbyes to one another. Peter held on until he had seen all of us. Daddy went back to Birmingham on Sunday. I received the call from Grady Hospital on Monday evening. A nurse told me, "There's been a change in your brother's condition, and we need you to come here immediately." Our little family was now minus one. I honestly feel that Peter was too good for this world. In spite of his addictive personality, my brother was flawless to me. Where he is now, matches who he really was... He is where he belongs, in Heaven with Jesus.

When Peter was dying, I prayed and asked God to please let him come and visit me one last time, but when he actually passed away, I remembered what I asked Him to do, and I realized that I would be very afraid. So, as I was driving home from the hospital, I began to pray and ask God to please not ever let my brother appear to me.

I say these things and speak about "What ifs" because I get very emotional when I think about my brother. However, I do know that everything that happens to us and all that we experience, whether good or bad, is pre-determined. The Lord is in complete control. Furthermore, though we may not understand why He allows the unfortunate trials, there is a reason. So, with that being said... Peter, I still miss you daily, and I will love and think of you forever. Last but surely not least, I hope that when you walked in through those pearly gates of Heaven, you immediately looked for and found our mommy. You just hold on tight to the end of her dress throughout eternity, Sweetheart. She'll never leave you. She and God will take very good care of you.

"The child I was is just one breath away from me."
Sheniz Janmohamed

I wanted to be near my sister and her family. She now had two baby boys. My oldest nephew was Kelvin James Reynolds, and his little brother was Brian Anthony. So, I moved farther up around The Perimeter to Stone Mountain. The apartment complex was large and wooded. It was an all adult community with a lovely ambience. It also had a pool with a fountain that reminded me of Paradise. I often went to the water by myself. However, it wasn't to swim. That was a skill which I never learned. My best friend, Jema and I took lessons several times, but we did not keep it up. Needless to say, eventually, I forgot what I learned. I just liked being in and around water. I enjoyed basking in the sun and reading a good novel. I suppose I got that from Jema. She was a tiny Caucasian lady, a few years older than me. She was pretty with long dark brown hair. She went to the tanning bed almost every day, and on the rare days that she didn't go, she loved to "Lay out" and soak up what the Mother Nature gave us. Jema didn't have a prejudice bone in her body. In fact, she lived in an apartment community on Memorial Drive in Decatur, Georgia. The vast majority of her neighbors were of ethnic background such as Iranian, Indian and African American. Anyway, in my complex there was a jogging trail which was perfect for my power walks and runs.

While I was living there, I received one of the best surprises of my life. In the year 1995 my telephone rang one evening. When I answered it, the voice on the other end said, "Hello Shirley"? I immediately recognized it and began to cry some "Happy tears," while loudly saying her name at the same time... "Aunt Bettye"! She giggled and began telling me how she obtained my number. She saw my father at her son's wedding. Daddy went there with Uncle Ben, and he gave her my number. She was my dear aunt who used to be married to Daddy's brother, Uncle Matthew. They moved in with us when my mother passed away. Her son was just a baby back then. Uncle Matthew passed away in the late 70s, but they were divorced even before he died. She was now married to Bobby Wortham, and they lived in the Dallas, Texas area.

Obviously, we had so much catching up to do. She wanted to visit me and my sister here in Atlanta, and we began to make some spontaneous plans. She came immediately. When I saw her, she was so very pretty, just like I remembered. She was just as short as I was. She had brown hair which is naturally curly, but she wore it straight with some curl on the ends. We all had the best visit ever. She came again during the Olympics, and this time she brought her husband Bobby with her. He was much taller and slim. We were able to spend some fun time in downtown Atlanta, making memories during this monumental time of my life. This was the beginning of several visits between me and her.

My sister and I now worked for the same telecommunications company. We were actually in the same department (Video), except I worked in the office, and she was a telecommuter, enjoying the benefits of working from home. Suddenly, she became ill and had to take some time off of work. Her symptoms were numbness and tingling in her upper torso. She also encountered problems with her eye which caused her to pay a required visit to an ophthalmologist- a specialist who studies and treats disorders and diseases of the eye. She underwent various testing with specific different physicians. Ultimately, she was referred to a neurologist- a specialist who treats diseases of the central nervous system, who then ordered an MRI- magnetic resonance imaging. Her final diagnosis was multiple sclerosis, commonly known as MS, a disease of the central nervous system. The problems she was having with her eye... well, that was optic neuritis. It's a condition that is frequently associated with MS. It's often, an early sign of it. Pain and temporary loss of vision are very common symptoms. She experienced both of these, and her problems actually lasted for several months before finally resolving themselves.

Even with her diagnosis of MS, I didn't realize the severity of this condition because we actually planned a week-long vacation to visit our relatives in California. Cynthia, Jema and I caught a plane to San Francisco. We took a Ferry to the City of Sausalito, where we walked the tourist area, bought some souvenirs from the shops and had lunch at a very lavish restaurant. We were seated near a large window with a scenic view overlooking the streets and the water. When we returned to the San Francisco Bay area, we rented a vehicle and drove to Antioch. This was the city where Uncle Ben and Aunt Noonie now lived. After staying with them for a couple of days, we drove up the coast, and stopped at Monterey Bay for brunch. Here, I had my first Mimosa. We spent the day in Hollywood doing the walking tour down Sunset and Hollywood Boulevards, then we took the Beverly Hills bus tour to see the movie star's homes. In the evening, we went to the Cheesecake Factory for dinner and visited a popular comedy club for entertainment. We did a lot of walking, and it didn't bother my sister at all. At least, she never said that it did. At the end of the night, we headed back to the hotel to get a good night's sleep because in the morning, we were driving to the San Diego Zoo. When we arrived at the zoo, we walked all day long viewing the animals.

My sister was blessed to have a very mild case of MS. In fact, she's never had problems walking or using her arms. She has had some serious optic neuritis issues, but to God be the glory, they were temporary. Other than that, she has some slight balance issues, and that is about it. When she was first diagnosed, to help put my mind at ease, she shared with me that multiple sclerosis was not hereditary. I would later learn that certain genes can increase the risk of developing the disease.

The year 1992 was truly of great sadness for me because alas, I experienced more than one tragedy. It was the year before when the telephone rang. I answered it, and on the other end was a Caucasian man who identified himself as a very good friend of Alton's. He first explained that he found me through the directory assistance. He knew my name because Alton spoke of me to him and his wife on many occasions. He said that Alton loved me and wanted to one day, marry me. He also said he told them that I lived in Atlanta. I listened carefully, without interrupting. This was hard to do because I heard heartache and sorrow in his voice. He told me Alton was involved in an automobile accident recently and was now in a coma. He and Alton's family thought my being at his side and letting him hear my voice, might make a difference and help to bring him out of this state of deep unconsciousness.

I immediately called his family to let them know that Alton's friends informed me of his accident. I asked if I could come right away. It had been almost 10 years since Alton and I were together. I saw him once, when I rode to Huntsville with my sister. She stayed with her friends, and Alton was kind enough to let me stay the night at his place. They were grateful that I wanted to be there for him and also, for them. Alton was very near and dear to my heart, and I would have done anything I could to help him. I hoped and prayed that my presence there, would help bring him back to us.

I've heard that people in a coma can hear the sounds around them. We were hopeful and believing that this was a fact. If what his friend shared with me was true, about the never-ending feelings he had for me, then hearing the sound of my voice just might give him the will and encouragement he needed to fight for his life.

I took I75 North and drove through Chattanooga in order to get to Huntsville. I thought it would be the quickest route. When I made it there, I drove to his parent's house. His siblings, the ones who lived locally, were there. It was wonderful to see them again. We left for the hospital shortly after I arrived. A few of us went into his private room. Hospitals aren't one of my favorite places. I try to avoid them. I've never been admitted to one, and I pray that it will never be necessary.

I saw him lying there. It looked as if he was in a deep sleep. He didn't look sick at all, yet he was unconscious. I almost felt guilty for thinking it, but he looked so handsome. His skin was flawless and his features, perfect. His face was model-ready, but his body was motionless. My mind flashed back to Baskin-Robbins when he and Maureen came in for ice cream. They were laughing and just playing around so lovingly. He was beautiful, and I couldn't get him off of my mind. Then my mind fast-forwarded to us when we were out dancing at BJ's Playground (a very popular local dance club on the South parkway) or at his home, in his den with his sister and her boyfriend. His friend Kaga was always there with us. Alton was such a good dancer. I was no match for him. When he entered the dance contests, he always partnered with another girl. I didn't mind. I was relieved that he didn't expect me to get out there on the dance floor with him to compete. Images from his modeling portfolio kept appearing in my head. I thought about his tender, French kiss and how his sister would tease us, and tell him to stop sucking my face. I remembered the letter he sent in the Manilla envelope and how in it, he said that he wanted to marry me when we are about 30 years old. I asked myself, why was I thinking of these things now because now, he is untouchable, unreachable and unresponsive? Earth to Shirley... someone was calling my name. "Do you want to come closer and visit with Alton?" said his mother.

"Yes of course." I leaned in and kissed his forehead. Then I softly told him that I was there, and I would always be there for him. I asked him to please wake up because we all wanted to talk to him. I held his hand. His feet were turned inward, and his toes were pointed at each other. I now know that was probably muscle spasticity or spasms. Well, he didn't wake up that time. However, that was just the first visit. There would be more. I was dedicated to helping him now, and I wasn't going anywhere. Since I couldn't be there every weekend, the nurses suggested that I make cassette tapes of my voice, so he could hear it often. So, I taped my voice reading scriptures, singing songs and reading passages from his favorite books. I would just talk to him about what was going on. I played his favorite songs like "Wind Beneath My Wings." He had given me a video of himself singing it for his family. I played some other more spiritual songs as well.

Alton was in a comatose state for three months. One day his sister called and told me that he was awake. Needless to say, I was on my way to Huntsville again. I called my supervisor to clear my schedule, grabbed my already packed stand-by bag and I was on the road. I was praying during the entire drive. I had recently told Daddy that I was double tithing. I was asking God for a modern-day miracle for Alton. Daddy had no comment. That meant he didn't agree with my thinking regarding the situation, but I did not care because my faith was strong. As long as I believed, that was all that mattered. After all, God woke him up.

When I arrived, his sisters wanted to prepare me for what to expect before I entered his room. They told me that I had to be strong because he wasn't the same anymore. There was severe damage to his brain and brain stem. Alton was now a quadriplegic.

He could not speak nor do anything for himself at all. I told them I understood, and I could handle it. I went in. The nurses dressed him in pajamas and a robe. They sat him up in a wheel chair. I walked up close so that I could talk to him. He made eye contact with me instantly, and I was certain that he knew it was me. I wanted to kiss his cheek, but I didn't. I was afraid to even hug him. He seemed so fragile, like he might break. I spoke words of encouragement to him. I let him know that I loved him and would always be there for him. I spent some time talking with his family about their plans to move him to a nursing facility in Tennessee. That broke my heart. Still, I promised to visit him and that, I did. One of his sisters told me to be careful because this was no time to fall in love with Alton again.

I continued to send the cassette tapes to his mother. She visited him every week. He was her baby boy. When I would visit, all of the nurses referred to me as Alton's girlfriend. They knew I was the voice on the tapes. They would bring him out to a private lounge area, and I would try to encourage and motivate him to do exercises with his fingers and hands. I would play games with him, similar to physical therapy sessions. For example, I would ask him to transfer marbles from one of my hands to the other. I could tell that he was trying to respond. He made a very good attempt to do it, sometimes almost succeeding. He struggled greatly because of the extremely extensive neurological damage. He had hardly any coordination, agility or control in his fingers. It was such a challenge for him to pick up and hold each marble. The fact that he knew what to do showed me that he was in there. He was trapped inside of his own body. It was a body which no longer worked and barely responded.

A long life here on earth was not in God's plan for Alton. About a year after the accident, he developed Pneumonia and went to Heaven to live among the other angels. He was about 30 years old. Rest in peace, my love.

Now that I was back in Georgia, with no more road trips ahead, it was time for me to get some much-needed rest and relaxation. I was extremely stressed, and I knew the perfect way to unwind and relieve the tension. I headed to the track, where I would hopefully be able to run and leave my sorrows behind.

When Daddy was 65, he received a diagnosis of diabetes. He experienced several minor strokes which were visibly undetected. However, they were causing him to have acute lethargy, vision and neurological problems that were affecting his hands, fingers, toes and his eyes. The neuropathy made it harder for him to play his beloved horn. In 1998, I received a disturbing call from Daddy. One day, he couldn't see clearly out of his left eye. So, they went to an ophthalmologist who referred him to The Eye Foundation. They referred him to the hospital to see a diabetic specialist who put him on insulin immediately and for the rest of his life. He lost the sight in his left eye. Five years later, he lost most of his right eye vision, except peripheral. He could see shadows. He described it as, "Being in the dark." He would add, "But I'm not completely in the dark." Daddy told me that his "Darling little wife" made him feel like he wasn't missing anything at all by not having his sight because she acted as his eyes. He said, "She describes everything to me in such detail." Daddy was always very positive and in such great spirits, even though he was blind. I would ask him, "How are you feeling, Daddy"? He always said, "wonderful."

Running was now a part of my daily routine. One evening, I was only there for 1 hour and 30 minutes, but it was time well spent at the track. I came home and sat down on the couch for just a minute. Before my shower, I thought I would grab my herbal supplements from the pantry. When I stood up and started walking toward the pantry, I felt something strange happening. It was like a vibration, a buzzing which began at the top of my spine or the base of my neck. It traveled down my spine, and when it reached my waist area, I immediately lost all feeling from the waist down. I dropped to the floor. Holding onto the door knob didn't help me. It was as if I had no bottom half, so the top was too heavy to hold up. How can you stand without legs, right? All of the feeling in my lower body returned after about five-eight seconds. I was in shock and disbelief.

I didn't know what had just happened, and I was so afraid of it happening again.

"Only the Good Die Young."
Unknown

CHAPTER 8
The Crushing Diagnosis

Unfortunately, it did happen again and again and again. In fact, this awful symptom occurred every time I awakened from sleeping in the morning or even from a nap on the couch. I was afraid to fall asleep in a chair, especially if I wasn't at home. It seemed to happen sometimes when I bent over... like once, when I was putting gifts under the Christmas tree. It was as if my spinal cord had a mind of its own, but then I guess it did because the central nervous system is made up of the brain and spinal cord.

It was the strangest and most devastating feeling that I had ever experienced. For the very first time in my adult life, I was afraid of something. Actually, it was the second thing because the first thing was... the dark. Honestly, I have always been afraid of the dark. I can remember back when I was a little girl (about five years old), my family would all be watching the television in our family room. The lights were turned off in the rest of the house. I was so afraid to go to the bathroom. When I finished, I would always come running back, while saying loudly, "A skeleton's after me."

With almost the same amount of anxiety, I was terrified of what was happening to me, and until I could find out what was causing it and how to correct it, I was going to be afraid to leave my apartment. What if it happened while I was simply walking in public? I became a recluse, a hostage in my own home. Except for work, I wouldn't go anywhere, and I couldn't help but think about it all day long while I was there because I needed to walk through the office. I remember having to get the courage to stand up and walk away from my desk and out of the workplace when it was time to leave at the end of my shift.

For as long as I could remember, I had been strong, brave and so independent. I was unafraid to go anywhere and do almost anything that I wanted and needed to do. Now here I was, petrified to cross the street or even walk the very short distance from my apartment to the laundry room with a basket of clothes. I was so afraid of losing all of the feeling in my legs and dropping down to the ground. It happened once, as I was walking from my vehicle to the building on my way into work.

I'll never forget it. I parked on the first level of the parking deck. There was a very long sidewalk with an uphill climb that led to the front of the building. As I began what seemed like would be a true journey, I was very apprehensive. When I reached the end of the sidewalk which was at the top of the hill, my worst fear happened. The buzzing vibration started in my brain. It was moving down to my brainstem. I knew that in a matter of seconds, I was about to lose the feeling in the lower half of my body and suddenly fall to the ground. Now my eyes began frantically searching for something... anything that I could quickly sit on. I wanted to cry, but I didn't have time. All of a sudden, I saw a tall cement block or a bench. I don't even know what it was or what it was meant for, but it was right there in front of the building. All I knew for sure was that God must have put it there for me. I sat on it. In as little as two seconds, all feeling left my lower half. I thought my legs were dangling, but I didn't know for sure because I could no longer feel them, and I was much too afraid to look down. In about five-eight seconds, all of the feeling that suddenly left my body, mysteriously returned.

As if this weren't enough, one morning I quickly got out of bed. As always, my feet hit the floor first, but when I stood up the entire room spun around me. The force of this sudden motion knocked me backward onto my bed. Now, when this incident happened, I knew without a doubt, that something very serious was wrong with me. This was actually my first experience with vertigo. I am so thankful that this frightening symptom didn't want to hang around. Vertigo is sometimes one of the earlier symptoms of multiple sclerosis. Some people have it frequently, and some do not have it at all. People who experience vertigo, usually do not drive because the vehicle or the road for that matter, might spin and this would be hazardous.

I have always been very inquisitive, so I decided to do some of my own research. I googled everything from stroke to brain tumor. However, the only disorder that seemed to address all of the same symptoms that I was experiencing was MS. So, I prayed that the Internet was wrong.

I began to feel dizziness which became more intense over the next several days. The fear of not wanting to hear her reaction to my bizarre symptoms kept me from calling my sister initially, but now I was ready to listen to her opinion. I called Cynthia, and as soon as I described the details of what was happening to me, she said, "You need to have an MRI." I said, "No, you think"? She said, "yes." I followed her advice and promptly called my HMO and scheduled an appointment. Unfortunately, I could not be seen until almost two weeks later. I was so anxious that I called back every day to check for the possibility of cancellations. That was the longest two-week period ever, and by the time my appointment date arrived, I was experiencing even more symptoms.

I had sharp pain behind one of my eyes along with double vision. In view of my sister's experience, I already knew that this was more than likely optic neuritis (if the worst-case scenario was to be my diagnosis). The other odd symptom was that my legs were both extremely heavy and weak at the same time. My initial visit was to my primary care physician. When I described my dizziness and room spinning symptoms, she wanted to treat me for kinetosis (motion sickness). I said okay. However, I also felt the need to inform her that my sister was diagnosed with MS three years ago. Therefore, I probably should have an MRI. She looked at me, this time nodding her head in agreement and said, "Yes, you're right."

She ordered a referral for me to visit a multiple sclerosis center. This is where I had my initial MRI. My neurologist displayed the microfiche on the wall for me to see the results, then he confirmed that I did have multiple sclerosis. My spirit was crushed. Although, my MRI did not reflect much activity, all I could think about was how I wished my symptoms matched my MRI because to me, it felt as if I did have quite a bit of activity going on. I was hoping the MRI would reflect a spinal disc problem or a pinched nerve or some other condition. I was praying that it would not be MS, even though the information which I found on the web indicated that it probably was MS. I wasn't that educated about the illness. I only knew that my sister didn't seem to have very many problems. Therefore, I claimed that my MS was going to be like hers. Even so, I felt like hearing this news today was the worst thing that ever happened to me.

I made a call to Daddy. I wanted to let him know that his "First born" had just been informed that she too, had multiple sclerosis. I didn't hear any surprise in his voice nor did there seem to be much concern. I felt hurt when our conversation ended because it lacked the warm, nurturing and encouraging words that I needed from my father. I wondered if maybe it was because he was going through his own health issues. After thinking about it, I didn't feel so wounded. I received a cassette tape from Daddy in the mail one day. He was playing "Girl from Ipanema" by Stan Getz on his saxophone. I believe it was his way of attempting to lift my spirits. On the note he wrote, to my "First born." He knew it would make me smile.

Once again, I went to the web. This time I was trying to find out as much as I could about this disease, and what caused my sister and me to have it. I wanted to educate myself, since I had to live with it. One of the risk factors is environmental. So, I wondered if the many chemical and manufacturing plants located in Huntsville contributed to it. I was also very curious about whether or not our diet as children which consisted of mainly processed and canned foods, played a part.

I have since read, that people should be really careful about disclosing medical information to their employer and co-workers. However, when I was initially diagnosed, I did exactly the opposite. I decided I was going to send an email to both of the supervisors in Video Technical Support where I was a technician. I informed them of my diagnosis and that I didn't plan on... needing any time off or missing any work. My supervisor replied, "Thank you for sharing something so sensitive and personal, Shirley." Needless to say, I felt kind of ignorant and a bit stupid at that moment.

It was unimaginable for me to have multiple sclerosis. Three months before I turned 40, my world changed overnight and would be different, forever. Things that I took for granted all of my life were now difficult for me. Things like stepping off of a curb because I suddenly had balance issues or standing up from a seated position on the floor or the ground was impossible, unless I had something to hold onto because of muscle weakness. There was no room for MS in my life. These two symptoms alone affected my ability to exercise effectively. Exercise had been so very important to me. No balance meant I would be unable to do sit-ups, crunches, and other floor exercises. I was taking step aerobics classes at my gym. That was going to have to end, at least for the time being. I hoped I would be able to pick that activity back up again later. However, that never happened. Eventually, and thank God not right away, I had to give up wearing high heels. I had a shoe fetish, but what girl didn't?

One of the first times I remember wearing heels after I began to regain strength back in my legs, was at church. I was a member of a well-known non-denominational megachurch in Decatur, Georgia. Surrounding our cathedral was a very large parking lot with steps leading to the building. I thought to myself, thank God for the hand rails. One Sunday after service, I was walking through the lot to my vehicle. My sister Cynthia was with me, and I remember smiling and announcing to her how happy I was because my balance and leg strength was improving. My heels had to be four inches tall. I purchased them right before I was diagnosed. I was determined to wear them, and MS was not going to stop me. I think that was when I first identified with the mentality of "I have MS, but MS doesn't have me."

Sleeping on my stomach was now so uncomfortable. I slept in this position for most of my life, but now I had to get used to sleeping on my side or my back. After a while, I could no longer sleep on my side because the muscle spasticity was now in my upper right arm. It affected my bicep and tricep muscles.

My mobility was affected right away because my leg muscles were severely weakened. Anyone who knew me at all knew that I looked forward to going to the track almost more than anything else. Exercise was a very important part of my life. I now had a phobia of losing the feeling in my legs and falling down in public. I could only walk on the treadmill for a short period of time because of my leg muscle weakness. Later on, the muscle spasticity made it difficult because the stiffness kept my right leg from bending, which made it hard for it to keep up with the belt, even when set on a very slow speed.

I began to ask God, "why" not why me, I knew better than that. The answer to that question was why not me? No, I just wanted to know, why? I thought of myself as a "good" person. However, the Holy Bible says...

Mark 10:18 NIV "Why do you call me good?" Jesus answered. "No one is good-except God alone."

I felt as if I had been given an unfair sentencing. I was an honest person, and I was much more than just decent. Did I always do everything right? Of course not, but who on earth was able to live up to that standard?

My father taught me good morals and values which for the most part, I lived by or at the very least, tried my best to honor within reason. I always treated people fairly and with respect, especially if they were my elders. I tried not to gossip, and I almost always refused to tell a lie. I made an honest living and was an example employee with a sincere work ethic. Except, for an occasional slip up in anger or when I broke a fingernail or stumped my toe, I almost never let a curse word pass through my lips. Of course, I'm not counting when I was a teenager or a young adult because like most people, those were my impressionable years. Oh, there were times when I might say something that I shouldn't, just to fit in, so I would be accepted and perceived as being hip and not square. Of course, I knew better, but at that time of my life it was more important to be popular. I'll admit, I was a little hot tempered when someone was rude, obnoxious or treated me unjustly, but if my behavior was unwarranted, I usually felt remorseful later and asked God for His forgiveness.

I allowed myself a glass of champagne on New Year's Eve. I had an occasional, Strawberry Daiquiri or a glass of wine at a restaurant or sometimes but not even all of the time, when I went out dancing. I liked Green Apple Martinis at Super Bowl. Other than on these mentioned occasions, I didn't indulge in alcohol.

Except, for the senseless brawl that Olivia instigated when we were roommates or arguments over silly things with my siblings or maybe a boyfriend, I never witnessed myself in combative behavior. I didn't steal and never tried to take anyone's life. I'll admit, my weakness was a handsome guy with long eyelashes, "Good hair" and a pretty smile. I allowed myself at least that one vice. For the most part, I was a loner. My friendship with Jema and a couple of platonic male friends that we hung out with was enough for me. Life was less complicated that way.

I never anticipated nor did I expect anything like this for myself. If I was experiencing problems with my mobility now, I couldn't help but wonder exactly what my future was going to be like. Honestly, I was terrified of the unknown, and because I lived by these standards, I did not feel that I was deserving of this life sentence.

Bernard was my most recent love interest. We met each other at the telecommunication's company where we both were employed. He was in my life just before the beginning of my MS journey. He genuinely cared about and loved me. To us, our romance was epic; but it was really just short and sweet. We had some good magical moments and amazing adventures that will go down in our history. After we ended it, we took a year to recover because our break up was intense. However, that emotional break really enabled us to develop a sincere friendship, and today I honestly think of him as one of my best friends. My friend has experienced some very similar debilitating symptoms which mimic MS. However, he suffers from totally different ailments. A herniated disc causes him to feel numbness, tingling, muscle weakness and some paralysis. He also lives with a condition called dumping syndrome. It can develop after stomach surgery. It happens about 15 to 30 minutes after eating. The symptoms usually include nausea, diarrhea, vomiting, weakness, dizziness, and fatigue. The latter three are like MS. Understandably, he could feel fine one hour and be sick the next. It is the same with MS. Unfortunately, I didn't always understand why we had to sometimes change or cancel plans due to his sudden illness. However, I certainly do now. In fact, we can laugh about it.

Multiple sclerosis is an autoimmune disorder, and the exact cause is unknown. There are theories regarding the cause, and the disease is not contagious. One can get MS at any age. The disease can affect the brain, spinal cord, and the optic nerve, which are all a part of the central nervous system (CNS).

An MS relapse happens when the immune system attacks good cells within the CNS because it thinks they are bad or foreign cells that are attacking the body. There certainly were times when I felt as if my immune system and my normal healthy cells were at WAR. During the earlier years of my MS journey, I had one to two relapses every year. This was definitely not a good thing because according to medical advice and my own inquiring research, a relapse may result in permanent damage. Hence, the reason for my changing disease modifying therapy's two times. I was taking an injectable named Avonex for the first few years. I then participated in a three-year clinical trial for an oral therapy called fingolimod which once approved, was known as Gilenya. Presently, I am taking a monthly infusion called Tysabri which I have been on for over five years.

I was used to wearing heels with everything. I didn't know what it was to not wear high heeled mules, sandals, stilettos, pumps, and boots. I didn't own any flats, except for sneakers, and I only wore them with shorts or to the track. I didn't even wear sneakers with blue jeans. For that matter, I did not buy outfits that I thought would go well with flats. Although, I am definitely not a depressed person, I'll admit that I was very disappointed when I had to give up my high-heeled pumps and stilettos which perfectly accented my cute little legs in a pair of pencil legged blue jeans. You see, back when I was younger and healthy, I was a legend in my own mind and probably no one else's. I told myself that it was okay to feel this way about myself because I felt like I deserved to... after being so shy, introverted and unpopular in high school and college. Besides, there was nothing wrong with having a little bit of self-confidence, and for me, it was about time.

I had optic neuritis which is inflammation of the optic nerve. It was painful, almost debilitating. My worst flare-up of this condition happened during a new hire training class. I accepted a position in a different department. The computers were mounted downward within the desks. Therefore, for six weeks my neck and head were fixed in this awkward position of looking down into the desk at the equipment. I had sharp pains behind and around my eye. It was the most uncomfortable experience ever. When the training session ended, all I could think about was that I made it through, and my God is so good.

Slurring was another one of my symptoms. I learned the art of keeping gum on the side of my mouth while being very careful not to chew. This kept my saliva glands stimulated so that I would not slur as 100 percent of my job function was talking on the phone.

I was experiencing severe muscle spasticity in my right leg and arm. It's a devastating symptom which I have lived with for almost 16 years. It's a very uncomfortable tightness and stiffness because my affected muscle is contracted and just won't relax. There are a few ways that I can experience a little relief from this condition. It makes me feel as if I am wearing a strait jacket and appear as if I have suffered a stroke. My arm wants to stay in a bent position toward my torso. One, is by taking a muscle relaxer named baclofen.

However, baclofen has a side effect of sleepiness. I have also created my very own soothing regimen for relieving the muscle tightness. I combine stretches which I learned from occupational therapy, with daily and nightly applications of a menthol muscle rub. I live by this plan, and it works. Thank God, in 16 years, I only had one more episode of vertigo, and it was very mild. I was at work at the printer... I had to hold on! I've never had another occurrence.

I experienced every single one of these bizarre symptoms almost instantaneously, and they were all happening at the very same time. Most of my symptoms lasted for months and some for over a year. I had never heard of a crazier illness.

Once my symptoms had settled down and I recovered from my relapse, aside from some minor adjustments which would end up being life-long changes, my existence for the most part went back to normal. However, the "normal" was a new normal. My life would never be the same. Unbeknownst to me, there would be many more relapses and many more changes.

MS affects each of its victims differently. Some people have a very mild MS which is referred to as benign MS, and others have a more aggressive and progressive MS. People with benign MS do not have many symptoms, and they may have a small amount of or no disability, even after 15 years. My sister has this type of MS.

On the other hand, I seem to have a more aggressive MS. I have more symptoms and limitations regarding my mobility. It wasn't always that way though. I remember back to when my symptoms were mild and invisible to others. She and I agreed once, that if this was all there was to MS and if it was only going to affect us in the small degree that it had so far, then we could surely live with this diagnosis. I didn't believe God gave this to me just because she had it, but maybe He allowed us both to have it so we could be there for each other and go through the journey together. In my heart, I still believe that is how God intended it to be. However, I've suffered a lot of progression, and giving God all of the glory, my sister's health has never declined. In fact, she is doing wonderfully today. I love my sister very dearly. However, she and I did have some problems in our relationship; unfortunately, we went our separate ways. We were estranged for about five years, but we are in each other's lives today. If God is willing, our relationship will only get better. I know we have the prayers of my parents, and prayer means everything.

Psalm 133:1 ESV
A Song of Ascent of David. Behold, how good and pleasant it is when brothers dwell in unity.

The very next month following my diagnosis, my sister, a couple of her girlfriends and I, planned a getaway to Panama City Beach, Florida. I readily wanted to go because the beach was my favorite destination. For that reason, I felt that walking on the sand and in the water, would be beneficial for my muscles, and the vacation altogether, would be therapeutic for my mind and spirit.

As we anticipated, the ambience was breathtaking. The palm trees and white sand which were in just about every view, were the perfect medicine for me. MS was new to me, or at least the official diagnosis was, so I was about to get a lesson on the do's and don'ts of living with MS while on vacation in the summer.

Once we were settled in our room which I made sure had a beach front view, we all went down the walkway to the beach so we could marvel at the sand and the water. Every time I visited the Emerald Coast, I was in awe of this miracle which God created. Each instance was as if I was viewing this wonder for the very first time.

I actually found myself reminiscing because being nostalgic is just a part of who I am. I was thinking about memories of me and Bernard in Destin Beach which was about 30 or so minutes down the road. We went there often. We really named it "Our place." I envisioned us riding the wave runner on the ocean. We would ride

157

together, then he would take pictures of me riding by myself. The first time we planned to go out on the ocean, I was really nervous. Bernard came up with the idea of going to the hotel's indoor pool to get me used to being in deep water. Remember, I wasn't a swimmer. He took me into the deepest water, which was about 12 feet, then he held onto me while I floated and became used to it. I'll never forget the victorious feeling I had when I finally conquered my phobia.

Bernard and I were quite adventurous. I remembered when we chartered a boat and went Deep Sea fishing at four in the morning. Out of four men and two women (six of us), little ole me caught the biggest fish. It was a beautiful silver King Mackerel. They even hung all of the fish up in order by size and of course, I stood proudly next to mine while Bernard captured my moment on camera. My catch was filleted right in front of us. When we returned home to Atlanta, I cooked it with butter, tomatoes, and onions, and it was one of the most delicious fish entrees I had ever prepared.

Since, the girls and I didn't arrive at our hotel until after noon, we decided that we would wait until tomorrow to put on our suits and enjoy the sun and water. We came down early the next morning to rent umbrellas, choose our spot and reserve our lounge chairs. This was necessary because all of the rentals filled up quickly. After having breakfast at one of the restaurants on the strip, we returned.

We spent the entire day in the sun, at the water. Of course, we were under umbrellas. My body is very sensitive to heat, and it makes my MS symptoms considerably worse. This is common for people with MS. However, I was able to tolerate the heat by being under the shielded shade of the umbrella, occasionally getting in the water and drinking cold fluids. Of course, that meant I had to be mindful of exactly where the restrooms were located because I would more than likely be making frequent visits. I am just as sensitive to cold temperatures. My muscles become extremely rigid in the chilling frigidness. I read and research whenever I have the opportunity, to ensure that I remain up to date and well informed on information concerning multiple sclerosis. More importantly, I do have to plan ahead. After all, I always want to be able to have the most enjoyable experience. I want to make sure I have an escapade that is without anxiety and unexpected difficulties.

It wasn't until we went shopping at one of the strip malls that I encountered problems. I found myself lagging behind, and they weren't waiting for me to catch up. Unable to keep up with Cynthia and her friends, the distance between us was rapidly increasing. My legs were feeling so heavy, yet they were also very weak. I was so confused. I didn't understand it. Ever since we left home, everything regarding my health was going so well, up to this point. I thought I was in control, but here it was controlling me. All of a sudden, I wasn't enjoying our excursion anymore. Instead, I was feeling sorry for myself. I didn't want this disease, and I didn't understand how God could want it for me.

Obviously, God had His own plans for me. After enjoying a nice dinner of salmon, shrimp and crab cakes on the lanai of one of the seafood restaurants on the strip, we returned to the hotel. I made a cup of orange tea and decided to go and sit by myself on the balcony because I wanted to seek my Lord, Jesus Christ. I looked up to the sky and saw the stars. I imagined that I could see right into Heaven. I asked God if He could possibly take this from me because it was going to interfere with my ability to be happy. When I thought about it reasonably, I could almost hear Him say to me (not in an audible voice of course but within my spirit), "I knew that you were going to be inflicted with this when I first created you. I cannot reveal to you, the outcome. However, I will tell you to stay very close to Me and hold on tight because you are in for the ride of your life."

"A cheerful heart is good medicine, but a crushed
spirit dries up the bones."
Proverbs 17:22

CHAPTER 9
Patiently Waiting for Mr. Right

BUT I'M NOT MARRIED YET! It was one of the first thoughts that ran through my mind after I received that very devastating medical report. When I was diagnosed in June of 2001, I was very single, and I did not have a special someone in my life. Marriage was not on my list of desired priorities. In fact, I was more than content with my "single" status. I was a very independent and self-sufficient woman. Of course, I dated, but I guess I had not yet met the man who I just couldn't live without or for that matter, couldn't live without me. If I had, he might have been able to persuade me to enter into Holy matrimony. Until now, I felt as if I had all of the time in the world, even though I was about to turn 40 years old.

I suppose it was now on my mind because I didn't know what to expect in my future. I wanted my destiny to include a wonderful and special person by my side. I needed someone who would love me unconditionally. I did not want to go forth on this journey all by myself. I did love before and it was reciprocated, but everything good doesn't always work out. I believed with all of my heart that God would bring that kind of love into my life again. This time it would be even better and also, everlasting. However, it would be in God's time, and I knew that His time was not the same as my time. I knew that I shouldn't try to rush God. Therefore, I had to practice patience. After all, He knew what I needed more than I knew myself.

I prayed about it almost daily. I asked Him to hand pick my husband, making him special… just for me. It was important that I recognize him so I wouldn't make a mistake and possibly miss the one sent from above. I tried telling Him what I wanted. Then I wanted whomever He wanted for me. So, I asked Him if He would just help my heart to receive him.

Since, I was in prayer about it, I felt confident that God was in complete control, and I tried never to dwell on it. However, I couldn't help but think about it from time to time. I was praying about it. Therefore, I was not going to worry about it anymore. My requirement was that he had to be a God-loving and God-fearing, born-again Christian. I knew he would be this kind of man if he were sent to me from my Heavenly Father.

On October 20, 2004, I wrote a Poem to God. I keep it in my mother's bible. I call it... My Prayer for My Husband

Dear God,
Let him be truthful and honest with me, about his present life
The one who will love me unconditionally
The one who will make me his wife
I've waited so long to meet him
I've prayed and trusted in Thee
I've been diligent, faithful and patient, as I promised I would
be
I'm asking for discernment, so my decision will be right
Then give me confirmation, when I pray to You at night
To be his love, his everything is the greatest hope I have
My reward for living righteously and walking in Your path
I trust in Thee for this promise, this desire of my heart
To bring us both together, until death we will not part
Amen

I was doing pretty well, especially for someone who had been diagnosed seven years ago. However, with each relapse, I lost a little something. The type of MS that I had was classified as, relapsing-remitting multiple sclerosis (RRMS). With this type, one has a relapse (attack), also called an exacerbation, and after a period of time, you go into remission. You may recover completely, or it may only be partial. In my case, I had experienced both scenarios. Unfortunately, several of my symptoms continued and did become permanent.

I can remember Bernard telling me a few years ago, "You need to get a cane." I was visiting him at his home when he noticed me holding onto to the walls. I laughed it off and replied, "I'm fine." Also, I fell a few times. Once, it was in the parking lot at my MS center. I was walking from my car to the walkway in front of the building, when I lost my balance and fell. Luckily, a good Samaritan helped me up and asked me if he could seat me in a wheelchair and take me to my clinic on the fifth floor. I graciously accepted his kind offer because I was a bit shaken up by the fall.

The second time I fell at a car rental office. This definitely was not my fault and unfortunately, could not be avoided. As I carefully climbed three steps and entered the office, I passed a couple with a toddler. For some reason, the baby decided to run after me. So, in order to avoid stepping on the child, I looked down. This caused me to lose my balance, which sent me crashing to the floor. The couple never apologized nor did they even acknowledge me. However, the employees went over and beyond, extending me their apologies and trying to ensure that I was okay.

The third time I fell was in my own back yard. I was standing in the grass while my doggie handled her business. For no reason at all, I lost my balance and simply fell on the lawn. This fall totally befuddled me. So, I made the decision to mention the incidents to my neurologist. He felt that it was very necessary for me to have a standard walker just in case I should ever need it, and he wrote a prescription. So, I exercised caution and had the walker delivered to my home that weekend, and I purchased quad and single canes.

I could see that my condition was worsening. I began to pray incessantly for my healing and the restoration of my health. I would read, quote and post scriptures on healing. I posted them on the insides of my pantry and closet doors, as well as on my bedroom and bathroom mirrors. I wanted everything I came in contact with to emanate positive energy about healing. Aunt Bettye gave me one well over a decade ago which I framed and have posted on my refrigerator door today. It has become one of my favorite scriptures.

Jeremiah 17:14 KJB
Heal me O Lord, and I shall be healed;
Save me, and I shall be saved,
For Thou art my praise.

I kept this same exact FAITH and continued to believe for my husband. I wanted to write another prayer to God. I knew He still remembered the first. However, now I had some new and different concerns, needs and desires. I saw a future ahead that I didn't want to face alone. I was actually afraid to face it alone. I was developing a disability, and I began to doubt that I would be wanted by a man, once it became obvious. I felt as if I was now unlovable. I thought of myself as damaged goods. I didn't know how I should pray or exactly what I should be praying for... Honestly, I wanted a strong and healthy husband, but would such a man ever be interested in me? Besides, I didn't want anyone to later, think of me as a burden.

The challenge was that even though I had this illness and my self-esteem was lessened, I still desired "Eye candy" in a mate. However, I also knew that nothing was too hard for my God.

So, I wrote... My Miracle

Dear Heavenly Father,
Please send Your Holy Spirit, to whisper in the ear
of a child of God who is worthy of me, someone who wants to hear
of how You want to bless him, with a faithful and loving wife
Someone who will always be by his side and love him for the rest of his life
I know You will be careful, to choose the perfect one. Then once we are together, You'll know Your work is done.
I believe with all of my heart and soul; our incomplete halves will become a whole. Thank You, Father. I love You so, for giving me this Miracle.
Amen

There were many counterfeits out there. So, I had to be mindful of this... and be very careful not to try and look for him myself. No matter how long it took, I had to patiently wait on the Lord, for He is forever faithful. I remembered His promise to give me the desires of my heart...

Delight yourself in the Lord, and He will give you the desires of your heart.
Psalm 37:4 ESV

I will wait for the Lord, my soul doth wait, and in his word, do I hope.
Psalm 130:5 KJV

CHAPTER 10
Changing My Mindset

Once again, I asked God, "why" because so far, the question had gone unanswered. When He finally revealed the answer to me, it more than satisfied my curiosity. Speaking to my spirit, He said, "I am allowing you to go through this because you're mentally and emotionally strong enough to handle it, and whenever you are not physically strong enough, I will always send someone to help you. Whoever leaves you, let them go. It will be okay because I never meant for them to stay for more than just a season. I will never leave you all alone. Even when you feel and believe you are alone, I will be there with you, and you will be okay." He also told me that He was going to use me as a testimony to others when He restores my health because He knows I will tell everyone... and I believed Him. I've honestly never asked God "why" again because I know that this is my assignment. I truly believe that this is part of my purpose, so I have to live it out.

I felt confident enough in what the Lord said to my spirit, that I actually decided to purchase a home in 2001, which was only six months after my diagnosis. It was a demonstration of my faith. However, I chose the wrong floor plan and the wrong area for that matter. I wanted to buy a home which was close to my sister's. This was the wrong decision because after only a couple of months, she moved away to Henry County. I was in Clayton.

Choosing a split-level foyer design was not a good idea and was one that I later regretted because I was beginning to experience some mobility issues. I really should have bought a ranch-style. I remember my sister asking me if buying a house with stairs was a fitting thing and I said to her, "This problem with my legs is only temporary." Little did I know that more contrary to my belief, this symptom was here to stay. In fact, over a period of time it became worse, but as it progressed, I didn't worry much or become afraid. I remembered that this was my assignment, and God was with me.

God also gave me the good common sense to think about either buying a stair lift or selling my house, and maybe consider it an opportunity to move out of Clayton County.

I attended The Cathedral of the Holy Spirit at Chapel Hill in Decatur. It was one of the nation's first integrated megachurches. I became a member there in 1991. While at the cathedral, I was involved in a few different ministries. I became quite involved in the AIDS Ministry immediately, in memory of my brother, Peter. It was the most rewarding time of service. There were only about six or seven of us in the group. It was a newly formed ministry. We would visit patients at Grady Hospital. It is the largest public hospital in Georgia, and it's located in Atlanta. We made baskets with fruit, nuts and candy. We would take them to the hospital and give them to patients during the week.

We met and befriended a man in the AIDS/HIV ward named Wil and prayed with him in his room. He was in his 40s, from the islands and he had no family here. In spite of whatever happened in his life that got him to this point, Wil had a very sweet spirit. We kept in touch with him, and we found a place for him to live once he was released. It was at a boarding house on Edgewood Avenue.

On Sundays, we took turns picking him up and taking him to church. It was winter, and the temperatures were cold. I remember that he wore a white towel around his neck. When I asked him what it was for, he said that it protected his face from the wind. So, I took off my black wool knitted scarf and gave it to him. Wil needed it. I could get another one. Usually, we all got together and shared a good meal with him after church before taking him back home. Sometimes, we took him to a restaurant and enjoyed a nice sit-down dinner. Other times, we picked up fast food like chicken or Chinese and ate it at one of our homes.

It made my heart so happy, knowing that Wil found God and gave his heart to Him before becoming very ill and passing away from AIDS-related problems. Even though we weren't there with him that day when he passed away, Wil didn't die alone because

God and His angels were with him.

I remember feeling quite a bit of anxiety each time I was faced with the challenge of going to the hospital and walking through the long hallways because of my mobility issues. Even so, I wouldn't have traded the experience for anything in the world. Witnessing the joy that we brought to this man's life when he had no one else, meant so much. Wil told me that he saw an angel once before. He said she was in his hospital room. After several seconds, he said, "It was you." I realized that in spite of all of my problems, I was so very blessed. God truly blessed us when He gave us Wil.

I was in the Book Store Ministry. However, I was very active in the Singles Ministry. I took my first cruise, and I actually found love once, in this ministry. Unfortunately, it didn't find me.

Willis was about five-seven, light-brown-skinned, handsome and very much in-like with me. We dated, spent time together often and I even met his father when he visited here from Seattle. Still, he chose to fall in love with another. She was a beautiful bi-racial girl with waste-length hair, and she wasn't "saved." Actually, she wasn't even in church. In fact, he met her at a nightclub and brought her to church.

When I saw them together outside of the sanctuary one Sunday, I was surprised and very saddened. I went home and cried. He didn't even tell me. After some time went by, he finally came over and told me about their plans. After dating for only eight months, they became engaged. He married her, and they moved away.

About 17 years later he looked me up and called me. Unfortunately, their marriage did not work out. He told me they were now divorced. He said she changed as soon as they married. She would leave him at home on the weekends and go clubbing with her girlfriends. Go figure. Even so, they stayed together for quite a while.

He was going to be in Atlanta soon. It was the same weekend as my oldest Nephew KJ's, high school graduation. He asked if he could escort me. I didn't see any harm in it. There were no sparks to ignite, at least not in my mind. So, I said, "Sure, why not"?

I wore a new spring outfit. It was a black and white flowered skirt and a capped sleeved black top with black heels. However, they were much lower than what I used to wear... only one and a half inches to be exact. We parked on the street because the ceremony was at the World Congress Center in downtown Atlanta. As we walked to the building, I held on tightly to his arm. He didn't realize it, but I was holding on to it for dear life because he was actually keeping me from almost losing my balance and falling. My equilibrium was so unsteady, and my legs were very weak. He probably thought I just wanted to be closer to him or something. I'm sure he thought my clinginess meant I was claiming him as my own. If he only knew.

He knew later when he tried to kiss me because my response or lack thereof, made it clear that there was no electricity. I almost felt sorry for him because he put so much effort into grilling steaks and lobster. He prepared an absolutely wonderful meal. He made baked potatoes, crab cakes and tossed salad, then he served it to me on the patio along with a nice merlot. It was very thoughtful and sweet. Unfortunately, it was about 17 years too late.

He called for a while, but with each call, I didn't anticipate nor did I look forward to the next one. Apparently, in his older age, he developed a very debating personality, and he would argue with me constantly. He debated about everything including the scriptures in the bible. I could not subject myself to this type of character. Stress is one of the most common causes of MS relapses or flare-ups. My objective was to eliminate all emotional stress and adverse or negative circumstances from my life. So, one day in a friendly way, I told him that we really didn't have that much in common, and that's probably why our conversations were so confrontational. I also told him that it was great reconnecting, and I wished him the very best.

I realized that I was feeling a significant amount of contentment in my life. My uneasiness and uncertainty about being alone was diminishing. I wasn't going to settle for anything less than the very best. I was going to wait for my God-given soulmate.

My period of worship at the cathedral was an important part of my life. I spent a great amount of time there every week. I attended services on Sunday morning and evening. There was a particular Tuesday morning service called "Life and Growth in the Spirit." It was held in the main sanctuary. However, it was a smaller, more intimate service. Occasionally, I would go if I wasn't working that morning, and I usually went to Wednesday night Bible study.

One special Tuesday I was off, and I decided to go worship at the morning service. I had not been in a while, and when I arrived, I learned that it was a new service and led by a different pastor. It was called "Healing Waters." I thought to myself, what a coincidence. The pastor began to pray, then she came out of the pulpit and down into the small group of people. She walked right up to me. She said, "I don't know what's ailing you, but I know you are in need of prayer." She touched my stomach while she prayed over me. I remember thinking... no, touch my head because my brain was in there. At the end of the service, she asked those who wanted prayer to come up front. I went up there. She went down the line praying over the people, and when she came to me, she smiled and said, "Well, I already prayed for you." I smiled and said, "I know, but I want more."

I believe that God brought me to that healing service to heal me of that devastating symptom where the buzzing vibration traveled down my spine and caused me to lose the feeling in my lower body. When in prayer, I said that I couldn't live with that symptom, and I asked Him to just take me on up to Heaven. After the service, I experienced the symptom for about six more weeks, then it left me. That was 16 years ago. Praise God it has never returned. So, you can't tell me that God doesn't perform modern day miracles.

1 Corinthians 10:13 "God won't give you more than
you can handle."

173

In the same year that I was diagnosed and bought my home, Daddy informed me that his older brother Uncle Ben, passed away. He was involved in a car accident. My aunt Noonie's account was that his injuries were severe. As a result, he was now a quadriplegic. He was unable to do anything for himself. He experienced heart failure, which per the physician, was very common for a patient in that condition. She told me that he was given the choice to live or die, and he chose the latter because he said he did not want to simply exist nor did he want to be a burden on his wife. So, my uncle left this earth. My aunt Noonie told me that 9/11 happened while he was in the hospital.

I was concerned about her and wanted to check on her. I was quickly developing courage. This was part of the armor which was necessary for my survival. My body felt strong enough, so I decided to go and spend some time with Aunt Noonie in Fresno, California.

The flight was 6 hours and 55 minutes long via Salt Lake City, Utah. Aunt Noonie let me use a buddy pass by means of Uncle Ben's survivor's benefits from the airlines. The flight was okay, except for having to catch the commuter plane. It carries passengers over relatively short distances. There was a lot of extra walking involved because I had to walk outside and directly up to the plane which was very small and had really limited leg room. These conditions were unfavorable for me because of the challenges that I had with my mobility and my occasional need to stretch my legs.

Fresno is in the center of the San Joaquin Valley, which is the Southern portion of California's Central Valley. The main attraction is Yosemite National Park. Once I arrived at the airport, my aunt was there waiting for me. She picked me up, and we headed back to her house. It was really great to see her again. She still looked the same, just as stunning as ever. She no longer wore the hairpiece that I remembered. However, she still had the most beautiful hair. She wore it pulled back in a small bun on the back of her head. She had on one of her colorful, flowing pants and tunic outfits and of course, her sandals.

The summer temperatures were just over 100 degrees in Fresno. I had to be mindful of the things that would keep me protected from the sun and heat. I made sure to pack a hat, sunscreen, and shades. I asked her to stop at the store, so I could get plenty of bottled water.

Her home was a cute three-bedroom stucco ranch. She had a lovely backyard with a very nice swimming pool. The yard was beautifully landscaped. It made me feel like I was in Paradise. It had some of the most beautiful tropical plants and pretty flowers. Uncle Ben had planted a peach tree. We could just reach up and pick one whenever we had a taste for the fruit. It was so juicy and delicious. It seemed as if everyone in Fresno had a gardener because each yard was always perfectly manicured. The neighborhood seemed like such a safe and friendly environment. It felt so different from Atlanta.

We spent a lot of time talking and reminiscing about my uncle Ben. We looked at photos, and she had many because they traveled and vacationed frequently. She told me that she had never noticed before now, how much I actually favored my uncle. We had cereal, juice and coffee by the pool in the mornings. In the afternoons, we visited her grandchildren. They were my second-cousins, and it was so nice to see them and meet their families.

I had the opportunity to have dinner with her son who was my first-cousin, at a nice restaurant. For dessert, he ordered Crème Brulee. It was my first time trying it, and I loved it, to say the least. Actually, it is now one of my favorite desserts. Afterward, he took me to see their ranch. He wanted to show me his man-made pond. It was populated with fish and some ducks. He even took me to get a tattoo. It's on my shoulder, and it was a mistake which I now regret. He and his wife had several on their arms. Some of them reflected very meaningful things like their children's names. Aunt Noonie and I met her girlfriends one morning, and we drove up to Table Mountain Casino where we indulged in our guilty pleasure. We didn't do any shopping at all. I guess it was no longer one of her enjoyable weaknesses.

It was the perfect, quiet and relaxing vacation that I needed, and I believed it was also good medicine for her. That's not to say that it was without MS challenges. As usual, my symptoms were in rare form and at all times. Fortunately, my MS was invisible to others. However, it was very noticeable to me. In fact, I always felt like MS was trying to control my body, at least the right side of it. I just refused to succumb to it. I still had a life to live, and I was not going to surrender to this enemy. The best way that I knew to fight back was to show this disease that I was much stronger than it was.

Grateful was the word that best described how I felt at the end of my vacation which seemed much too short. I was so thankful to Jesus that I was able to create a little happiness in Aunt Noonie's world. I realized that when I stopped focusing so much on my own problems and instead, noticed someone else's needs, I was not only much happier, but my worries temporarily disappeared or at the very least, were minimized. Empathy has always been one of my strong qualities. I first demonstrated this essential trait when I was concerned about how my father must have felt when his dear friend left, after he relocated us all of the way across the country from California to Alabama.

I became very compassionate about other people. This was why I enjoyed volunteering for the types of ministries which helped the underprivileged, such as the AIDS Ministry. My involvement in this ministry was life changing. I was busy doing things to help others who were not only less fortunate than I was but who had an illness that might have been even more devastating. I didn't have the time to feel sorry for myself or give too much thought about how tired my heavy legs were because I was busy caring about them and trying to come up with ways to make their world a little bit brighter. I developed into a more kind and considerate person. My life was more fulfilled. Try not to be so centered on your own life that you're unconcerned about those around you. Be more charitable... not only will you feel better, you'll probably be a better person. I hope others notice because I'd like to be a positive example to them.

I was blessed with the most rewarding assignment from God one February. I had an idea. I asked my sister if she would like to get together with me and make sack lunches to give out to the homeless for Valentine's Day. She wasn't able to, so I didn't think much more about it. Then one day I suddenly received an email from a ministry of women. I didn't know of them. However, they were asking for volunteers to make lunches for the homeless for Valentine's Day. We could sign up for the items we wanted to contribute, and we were going to meet to make the lunches. I thought to myself, how awesome. I think I brought chips.

We made peanut butter and jelly sandwiches and added a cookie and the chips. We put a Valentine's card in each brown bag, then we trailed each other out to some of the interstates. We went to the overpasses because they lived under them. They had camps set up underneath the joints of the highway. We were going to walk up the base which looked like a small pyramid, to get to their camps. I was apprehensive at first. I had never done this before. However, the others had. I said a prayer and asked God to please strengthen my legs and protect me. I began to walk up. It wasn't as scary as it looked, and before I knew it we were up there.

I felt so favored to be witnessing this and just to be a part of it was a miracle. I thanked God for this experience. Most of the people weren't home. We found several open bibles next to their beds. We would leave a lunch next to them. After visiting a few highways, we went downtown to a shelter and handed out the rest of the lunches. I had never felt so blessed. I came home and wanted to tell everyone I knew. I called Daddy first. He was excited to hear all about my experience.

I was in my new house when Aunt Bettye, her husband Bobby and her two granddaughters came to visit for the Fourth of July. They drove here from Dallas and stayed with me for the entire week. I enjoyed their visit so much and just loved having them here in my home. Making breakfast for all of them was such a pleasure. I remember being in my kitchen cooking bacon, waffles, grits and eggs... served with juice for everyone. My legs did feel heavy and fatigued. However, that was now normal to me.

Each day we picked up my nephews KJ and Brian and went to a different attraction to experience an enjoyable and exciting new adventure. I had so much fun showing them my city. We went to the World of Coke, Underground Atlanta, Centennial Park, The Martin Luther King Center/home and Stone Mountain Park. We walked the park with its many blocks and trails. We hiked some parts of the mountain. We visited the mansions with slave quarters. There were rides including a Skylift, and in the evening, there was the world's largest laser show with a finale of fireworks. Absolutely, it was a bit tough and strenuous on my legs, still I wouldn't have done it any differently.

I decided that I was going to travel to as many places as I could and do as many things on my bucket list as I wanted. MS was trying to take away my mobility. I was faithful in believing that it would not happen. Even so, I wanted to ensure that I fulfilled some of my dreams. One of my biggest regrets is that I never went to Hawaii while I was healthy. I've always wanted to go there. I haven't given up on it because I believe that through research, a method will be found to reverse the damage that has been done. I believe it will happen in my lifetime. The scientists are diligently working on this.

My sister and I were involved in Mary Kay Cosmetics. She was a director, and I was a sales consultant on her team. The company has an annual convention in Dallas, Texas, and I wanted to experience it for the very first time. I anticipated that it would be somewhat challenging. However, it more than tested my abilities. We walked everywhere wearing heels because we were dressed in our complete MK uniform at all times. I was unaware of exactly what to expect. However, I was committed to attending the mega sales and training meeting. I know that it was my positive attitude and unwillingness to give in to the pressure that enabled me to get through the entire experience, and it was a wonderful experience indeed. Anyone who has been to a Mary Kay Convention knows exactly what I mean.

While at the convention, I met a guy. He invited me to lunch for Sushi that day. I liked Micah and was very interested in getting to know him better. Unfortunately, I had to decline because we were leaving to catch a flight back to Atlanta later that afternoon after the seminar. So, we just exchanged phone numbers. He did call, and we talked, quite frequently.

I visited Aunt Bettye and her husband Bobby in Dallas, Texas a few times. The first couple of visits were fine and without an MS incident. They were always the most wonderful visits. Their home was a brick ranch in a beautiful, well-kept neighborhood. We would visit my second cousins, and their dad (my first cousin), always came over. We did some walking around downtown, but nothing presented itself to be too difficult for me.

My first visit was such a blessing. I remember that we hugged each other and cried happy tears together. I love my aunt so much, and she knows it. However, I don't know if she has any idea just how much. I've loved her ever since I was a little girl, when she and my uncle moved in after my mother passed away. When I was 10 years old, Peter, Cynthia and I, spent a few weeks with her, Uncle Matthew (Daddy's brother) and my cousin who was a toddler then, in Los Angeles. Aunt Noonie and Uncle Ben, who we were visiting in San Francisco, probably appreciated and welcomed the break. She had a girlfriend who sometimes came over in the evenings when my uncle was working. This was their "Girl Time" together, yet I remember feeling a little jealous. I guess I didn't want to share her with anyone.

Micah was about five-eight, with a slim yet muscular build. He was handsome, a product of a mother who was from India and a father who was Black. His complexion was light brown, and if he had hair, you could tell that it would have been a nice texture. However, he wore a completely shaved head. Micah and I decided to see each other again. We wanted to spend some time together in Dallas. So, the next time I visited my aunt, we went out.

He picked me up at their house, so he met her and her husband,

Bobby. He was taking his niece to a fair, and he invited me to join them. We did quite a bit of walking around. Keeping my balance in "Stacks" which were popular again, was challenging. Nonetheless, I still had lots of fun. We went on a few rides and played some games, giving her the opportunity to test her skills and win some prizes. After we had taken her home, we realized we were both hungry. What do you think we decided to eat? We were finally able to have that meal at a Sushi restaurant, after all. He took me home, walked me to the door and kissed me good night on the forehead. I thought it was nice, and he was a perfect gentleman.

The next day, Aunt Bettye and I went to her megachurch. I was privileged to attend services at the well-known, Oak Cliff Bible Fellowship. It is a 10,000-member church, pastored by Dr. Tony Evans. On our way home from service, I received a call from Micah. He and his best friend Floyd were taking Floyd's boat out on the water. He asked if I would like to spend the day with them. I accepted his invitation. He picked me up, and we were on our way to meet his friend. I had no idea that I was about to begin an excursion that would be the most fun I've ever had in my entire life.

Floyd was tall, about six-two, and he probably weighed over 300 pounds. At first because of my MS, I didn't know if the outing was going to be a positive experience or not. To get to the boat, we had to go down a dockside walkway. Of course, they allowed me to go first. This was the one time when I wished men believed that chivalry was dead because I would have given almost anything to be walking behind them instead of in the front as my legs felt like jelly, if you can even imagine that. I knew they were looking at them as I walked because that's just what guys do. The thing was that it was impossible for me to try and walk cute, when I didn't have that much control over them. Then I had to jump down into the boat. I thought, oh my God... what did I get myself into?

Once I was on the boat, everything was smooth sailing. The beautiful ambience, music, fun, laughter and incredible company of these two friends who were like "Frick and Frack," made this pleasure voyage, simply unforgettable. The sun, the waves and just the experience alone, of being in the boat on the water was so exhilarating. I'll never forget how we got such a kick out of it when Micah and I sang "Cater 2 U" by Destiny's Child to each other because amazingly, we both knew every single word. Afterward, we gave each other a high five, and we all laughed incessantly.

Aunt Noonie called and invited me to meet her and her dear friend and roommate Andy, in San Antonio, Texas. She told me that my aunt Bettye and her granddaughters were also coming from Dallas and meeting us there. We had the best time. It was one of my most favorite vacations. On our first evening, we all went to a restaurant known for its good food and entertainment. A friend of mine had an R&B band that played there. I met him in St. Louis, Missouri when my high school band played for a Cardinals game. We kept in touch over the years. So, I surprised him by making reservations. I requested a table for six near the stage, so we would have a really good view of the band. When he saw me, he was pleasantly surprised and came over to ensure that it was me. We embraced and laughed because he could hardly believe it was really me. Then he called each of his band members over one by one and introduced them to all of us.

There was a small dance floor in front of the band. Although I wanted to dance, I was too apprehensive because I wasn't confident about my balance or physical agility. It was a challenge even to stand up and walk to the restroom which wasn't very far from our table at all. However, seeing my friend after all of these years and witnessing him in his element-performing with his own band, was something that I was determined to do while I was able to do it independently without an assistive device. And I did it! On this night, there were four generations of Merritt women present at our table. The band put on an awesome performance, and it was the best night ever.

My family and I spent the next day out on The River Walk. It is a tourist attraction for shopping and dining, walking or enjoying a river taxi ride, and it was right outside of our hotel. I was so glad I went on this getaway because in spite of the difficulties which I tried never to consider to be major, I enjoyed it immensely.

Aunt Bettye soon called me and invited me to meet her and her grandsons (my second-cousins) in Fresno. We were all going to stay with my cousin and his wife on their ranch. They already made plans for all of us to go visit Yosemite National Park. I did encounter some difficult situations concerning my mobility. I found myself being unable to maintain my balance very well. I felt like a child who was learning how to stand and walk. I was very grateful for my aunt Bettye.

I wondered if it was my imagination, but she seemed to stay close to me. She didn't verbally tell me this, but it seemed as if she wanted me to know that she was right there in case I needed her. As we took steps and moved around, she would slightly reach out with her arm and hand, just in case I needed to hold on. I appreciated her caring and kindness so much. I was beginning to think that I might have to start using a cane or even the walker soon.

I was learning a great lesson in humility. This was a noun I often associated with myself. My daddy always thought of me as meek, and sometimes he reminded me of this. I guess I could sometimes see the submissiveness in me. I was definitely not a prideful person. My character was humble, and I believed those who knew me would agree. Humility is a necessity for Christians. However, I wasn't lacking in an allowable amount of vanity, and I have always thought of myself as assertive, whenever I wanted or needed to be.

That was the only time we parked and walked around. The rest of the trip was spent driving up the mountain, stopping to see the rock formations and waterfalls and just enjoying the view, then we drove back down. After that excursion, we went out to eat at a Chinese all you can eat buffet, and because of that mind and body exertion, I really did work up an appetite.

When we made it back to the ranch, I went out to the pond to daydream. It was peaceful and a perfect place in which to meditate or at least engage in very deep thought about something of great importance. I decided to go over the qualities which I perceived as positive that I possessed in my own heart. I did this often and still do it today. I want to keep checking myself in order to ensure that I remain deserving of the healing miracle which I am asking of God.

Independence and self-sufficiency are qualities which identify me. I realized that I was going to have to get used to accepting assistance from others. I am honest, trustworthy, truthful and sincere. I am reliable and dependable. I am a loyal friend who will be there to the end, with unconditional love. Truly, I care about people and have genuine empathy for them. Yes, I try my best to be thoughtful. I am always thinking of others and what I can do for someone. I find it very easy to be forgiving. This is one of the most important and invaluable qualities because in order to be forgiven by God, we have to forgive others. I believe in being respectful and gracious. Having these good qualities means everything to me, and it is so very important that I try to hold on to them because I want to always be pleasing to God.

This vacation was just like a mini-Merritt family reunion, and I wouldn't have missed it for the world.

I took a good look at my heart to see what I regretted the most in my life. I regret that I never had children. I never felt as if I was missing anything, but I do now, for family means everything.

If you have a loving family, you are RICH!

"Family is Life's Greatest Blessing"
Unknown

186

188

CHAPTER 11
I Can Do All Things Through Christ Who Strengthens Me

Layoffs, downsizing, and outsourcing were common terms that were used in corporate America during the early to mid-2000s. Unfortunately, the telecommunications company I worked for was no exception. It seemed as if almost every year we were facing a layoff. My sister's employment status had already been affected. I wanted to have a backup plan in case the same thing happened to me, so during the summer of 2006 I decided that I was going to follow Daddy and Cynthia's footsteps and obtain my real estate license. I enrolled in the Georgia Multiple Listing Service (MLS) Training Institute. The course wasn't very difficult, still there was definitely a lot of information to learn.

I was 45 years old, and it had only been five years since I was diagnosed, yet it was already challenging for me to walk through the office just to get to the classroom. I thought, surely, I must be having another relapse. The worst part of it was that after finishing an assessment we had to take our paper up to the very front of the classroom and put it on the instructor's desk. Now, I know this task doesn't sound so hard, but what made it difficult for me was that we had to walk up two steps in order to get to it, and that was very intimidating because I had nothing to hold on to. Needless to say, I dreaded exam day. I only wished it could have been for the same reasons everyone else did. I spent unnecessary time thinking about how I would manage that feat, when I needed to use that energy for concentrating on the test.

At the end of the course we waited after class to receive our final grades. I was delighted to know that I did very well and successfully completed the training. I could now take the Georgia Real Estate License Application. I had a fixed deadline to apply for a license by September 27, 2006, but I applied sooner. On June 27, 2006, I passed the certification and was a licensed salesperson. I entered into an agreement with Keller Williams Realty and leased office space with them for several months, maybe even close to a year, where I struggled to even be visible. I faced mobility challenges daily that were invisible to everyone else. To others, I appeared to be normal. However, to myself, I was anything but... I could have chosen to continue to pay fees and stay current with the required certifications. However, I succumbed to my ominous circumstances and allowed myself to go into an (Inactive) status. I suppose I didn't have quite enough faith. I was reasoning, instead of using my "new mindset" because according to it, I will walk without any problems one day.

The pastor of my church passed away in 2009. I attended his funeral, as did many of my friends from the ministry. I arrived early. I wanted to ensure that I would be able to select my seating but more importantly, a good parking space. As members and former members entered the sanctuary, I recognized faces, some of whom I had not seen in years. I suppose everyone who had ever been a member of the congregation and some who had merely attended services at Chapel Hill, came to honor the Bishop and pay their respects at his funeral.

Immediately after the service, all of the people walked behind a horse-drawn carriage that carried the casket of the Bishop... that's what we called him "Bishop." Two of my dearest friends who sat near me inside, wanted to assist me so I could be able to take the walk with them behind the carriage and around the cathedral. They were both strong men. One held onto my right arm and the other, to my left. They sort of lifted me with each step that we took. They ensured I did not fall. I was so very thankful and grateful for them. They really blessed me that day. It was because of their kindness, empathy, and helping me to walk, that I was able to take part in the tribute to our Bishop Paulk.

God has given me more blessings than I could ever ask for. In fact, He always knows exactly what I need, before I even ask. There are so many times that he blesses me, without my even asking. This time I was asking for more than just a blessing. What I needed was a modern-day miracle, and believe me, I knew that He would provide, if it were His will because He had done it many times before. Later after I returned home, I realized there was something I had to face. It was that walker which was in a closet downstairs. I hoped I could keep it there, never having to remove the cellophane in which it was wrapped. I prayed that this place where it was stored would be its permanent home. However, my balance was becoming very unstable, and now my right leg was really beginning to drag. Although I surely did not want to give power to these thoughts, I wondered if what I had experienced at Yosemite and the Bishop's funeral, was indicative of my future.

I was more than thankful for the gifts I had received. As of my diagnosis, I was blessed to spend quality time with my family and friends, enjoying a cruise and carefully planned vacations that we can cherish forever. We made memories that will last a lifetime. Although there was much more travel on the agenda of my bucket list, I was doubtful that I would be able to realize it anytime soon or in the near future because of the present decline of my condition. Right now, I felt the crucial need to put everything I had into some important and very necessary rehabilitation.

I was now working as a telecommuter from my home for the telecommunications company. I purchased a desk, a chair and a cabinet and turned a downstairs bedroom into my office. We were sent home one by one. This process ensured that if in the instance, one of us had problems connecting to the network, it would not affect the efficiency of the entire group.

To be able to wake up, put on some very comfortable clothes, eat breakfast, and sign into the phone system by eight o'clock... all without leaving my home and driving through heavy Atlanta traffic, was definitely one of the best blessings God had ever given to me. I held onto this position which was a perfect situation, for about five amazing years. I had the very best supervisor. She knew of my challenges, for I confided in her about the MS. I once told her that she was like an angel that God had watching over me.

I had an appointment Monday morning with my primary care physician. I planned to take my standard walker for support. It would be my first time using it. Almost as soon as you leave the building there is a downhill stroll to the parking lot. I anticipated that I wouldn't be able to make the decline without the assistance of a walker. Walking uphill to enter the building took little or no additional effort. Therefore, I did not have to rely on the aid of the equipment. However, the outcome was totally different when it was time to return to my vehicle.

I opened the walker, and immediately as I began to descend downward, a feeling of relief and then one of gratitude came over me. I was suddenly so very thankful for the walker. I braced it and was able to put all of my weight on it. It was holding me up. I was able to walk. I moved without thinking about it. This was an act I had been unable to do without carefully concentrating. Not so long ago (like only 45 minutes), I had to look down at the ground and at my feet. I was calculating my steps in order to ensure that I did not mis-step. What was even worse, I might trip up and fall. It was as if I noticed the trees and flowers for the very first time. I could look directly into people's faces, smile and say hello. I wanted to immediately drop to my knees and give thanks to God for giving me this blessing. However, I knew that if I did, I probably would not be able to get back up unless some kind do-gooder stopped and helped me. So, I decided to do the wise thing which was to humbly carry on, making my way to my vehicle. Little did I know, when I followed my doctor's advice and had this walker delivered to my address, I was making one of the best decisions of my life.

Lately, I hadn't been such a good and attentive friend to Jema. Unfortunately, I was so very focused on everything else such as my current male companion, family and traveling and now this illness which I was trying to be careful not to claim as mine anymore, that I neglected Jema and her very loyal friendship. I lost my buddy and my best friend because she soon moved away to Charlotte, North

Carolina. It was 244 miles away from here. I had wished she would return so we could be roommates because she's one of a kind and irreplaceable. However, it was not in His plan. Our God was in control because she actually met the love of her life, and they are now married. I am so very happy for my friend, Jema.

Ironically and for the time being, the walker, a device that I once, refused to look at, was now my new best friend. I relied on it for everything. It was needed to take me everywhere. I was so reliant on it that using it became second-nature. I was certainly never ashamed of it. Yet, I felt a kind of uncomfortable embarrassment if I suddenly ran into someone who knew me in my previous life. You see, I thought of this life that I was now living, as my new life. At first, I didn't quite know how to handle the suggestion that I seemed to be so rapidly becoming disabled. Understandably, I would not accept the idea because with a positive mindset like mine, this was not supposed to happen.

In the beginning, I believed it was just a severe relapse that would eventually get better as time went on. However, with each year that came and went, it never did. So, in order to keep from being depressed about it, I developed a fresh way of looking at it. I would get very busy, spending my time and energy involving myself in things such as activities associated with MS during the week.

I drove to Huntsville to visit my daddy and Lula one weekend because I wanted their advice. They moved back there after they retired from their ministry in Birmingham. I took I-75 N and went through Chattanooga.

Daddy had been blind for years now. He once told me that Lula made him feel as if he wasn't missing anything by being blind. That is the nicest thing I have ever heard anyone say about anyone else. He was sitting in a chair across from me. Lula and I were on the sofa. Their apartment was very humble. Lula's decorating style had always been very modest and simple. As we were all engaging in conversation, I noticed that Daddy's eyes were turned upward, as if they were looking at the ceiling, then I immediately remembered that he still had peripheral vision in one of his eyes, and that was probably the reason why.

I talked to them about my thoughts of retiring from my company and going on disability. They definitely understood and supported my thinking. It was emotional for me because 24 years is a long time. I felt as if I'd always worked there. I did feel relieved after talking my decision over with them. It was a short visit because I didn't intend to stay long. So, after a few hours I headed back home to Atlanta. I decided to take I-65 to 20 East. I was sort of in the mood to drive through my old stomping grounds... Birmingham, for some reason.

I remember it well... the day I went into my neurologist's office and asked one of the ladies at the front desk if I could speak with the case manager. As soon as she walked up to me, tears came out of my eyes. She suggested that we sit down. I explained to her that I was ready to stop working because it was becoming much too difficult for me. I asked her if I had that option. She told me that I did. She explained the process we would follow, and if I was ready, we could get started immediately.

Leaving my place of employment after 24 years of service and going on disability, was one of the hardest things I have ever had to do. Although, it was unwanted, it was necessary, and it was time. I was blessed because I continued to work for 11 years after I was diagnosed. It was because of my faith and God's good grace that I was able to efficiently and proficiently maintain my positions with my employer.

I was relieved that while I worked all of those years, I was smart and followed my good common sense. I enrolled in a supplemental short-term disability policy which was paid for via payroll deduction of a very small amount. This was really helpful because most companies will only pay a percentage of your income, and mine paid 75 percent. However, because of the STD policy, I received an additional check each month for almost the same amount. Of course, my long-term benefit was automatically paid to me after six months by my company, then my actual social security disability benefit started. I was now separated from my company, and it was a very peculiar and unfamiliar feeling. I hoped it would leave me soon. I didn't want it to hang around.

Now that I had received my standard walker which was paid for by insurance, I purchased a second one out of my own pocket, so I would have a back-up. Having two came in handy because I could take one inside of the house and leave one in my vehicle. I also bought a rollator and used it for outdoor long-distance walking. A rollator is heavier and has larger rubber wheels. It has a seat and a basket or a compartment for storing items. It also has breaks which lock, keeping the equipment in place and from moving.

I never even anticipated having to use the walking aids for an extended period of time, as I mentioned earlier. However, things don't always turn out the way we would like them to, so I was grateful to have these assistive devices. Without them, I would have been home-bound. I had a lot of will and desire to get out and still be able to be around people, doing the things that made me happy. My mindset was I may be disabled but I didn't plan on always acting like it or living that way.

I loved to shop, but even a rollator was not going to help me get through a mall. The last time I tried to was when my dear friend from Huntsville came here to shop with her daughter for school. She was going to be a senior, and she wanted to buy shoes at Macy's, so we went to a nearby mall. It was a smaller mall, so I wasn't intimidated. However, I soon realized that keeping up with them took much more effort than I anticipated.

The department store had a sale, so she found some bargains. My friend encouraged me to try on a pair of heels. She noticed me admiring them. I said, "I cannot buy them because I would never be able to wear them." She said, "Just try them on anyway." You see, we had been friends since childhood. She was the one who had a disability. Although, nothing about her mindset revealed that she was disabled. I was a teenage bridesmaid in her wedding.

She was now a minister, and I was at the ceremony when she was ordained. She wanted me to exercise my faith. She told me to put them on and stand in front of the mirror. As I started to shake my head no, she said, "It's okay, use your walker for support." I did it, and when I saw my reflection it reminded me of the past. Then she said that I should purchase them and call them my "FAITH" shoes. The shoes were on sale for only 49.99, so I bought them. Later, I put them on and took a picture. I show them to people sometimes, and I honestly do call them my "FAITH" shoes. I haven't been able to wear them yet. However, I truly believe that one day I will. I am so proud of who my friend has become but then she's probably always been that way.

The muscle spasticity in my right leg was quite severe, and the weakness made it heavy. It felt like I was carrying dead weight. My physical therapist educated me on this symptom. She informed me that when a muscle is weak, it feels heavy.

I decided to call the malls in the Atlanta metro area and find out if they had chargeable scooters. Surprisingly, I found them only at one mall. The good thing was that the mall happened to be located near me. Unfortunately, they only had one unit that was operable. However, I was fortunate enough to be able to get it almost every time I wanted it. I assumed not many people knew about it, and all that was required, was to leave my driver's license there with mall security. Regrettably, I found out the hard way that I should first make a copy of it, in case I was required to provide it when making an applicable transaction.

The first time I utilized this service, I had such a positive and memorable experience. I asked the security personnel how long I could use the scooter, and he said, "For as long as you'd like to." I thought, well now that wouldn't be fair to others. So, I was quite considerate and returned it in a few hours. I did some much-needed shopping, as well as purchased a few items that I just wanted. I even treated myself to a deserving, self-indulgent experience at Victoria's Secret, where I purchased fragrances and some lovely feminine undergarments.

Before returning the scooter, I went to the food court to get lunch. So many new restaurants had been added since the last time I was there a few years ago. It was the summer season, and I couldn't resist leaving with some barbecue. I helped myself to a pulled pork sandwich with sides of sauce and Cole slaw. I would add them to the sandwich after I arrived home.

This was the day I decided that I must own one of these devices myself. So, I immediately contacted my insurance company and made the appointment for "seating." The medical assessor, sales representative and myself, met at the designated seating clinic at Shepherd Center, where it would be determined if my condition warranted their approval of my request. It did, so they wrote it up and submitted it to my insurance company. Needless to say, I was on pins and needles while giving my best attempt to patiently wait.

Going back to that day when my lone outing was over, I felt such a sense of freedom, accomplishment and independence. It was so enlightening to know that there would be more of these shopping excursions in the near future. You see, it was others who felt sorry for me, but no... I never did. All I needed was to be shown one time that I could do something on my own, and then I would RUN WITH IT! Of course, my Maker already knew this about me, for He created me to be a loner. This wasn't something I acquired. I had always been this way. I remembered what He told me about feeling all alone. He said that He would be here with me. This was all of the assurance that I needed. Those words fueled my strength and gave me the encouragement, energy and strong will to keep going and to never allow myself to be so overwhelmed that I would give in and stop.

Now, don't get me wrong. This journey isn't over. I still believed God was going to heal me and be assured that I'm still believing it today. However, the Lord was sending me some assistance, for I needed help along the way. A beautiful candy apple red scooter was delivered to me. I keep it charged and ready to go.

About one year later, my insurance approved 24 sessions of physical and occupational therapy. It was 12 for each classification. The physical therapist wanted to try a piece of equipment on me to see if it would improve my gait (the way I walk). She explained that this device could help me to regain function in my lower leg and foot which did not want to lift. More often than not, it dragged. The condition is called foot drop. Although, in my opinion, it should be called... leg drag! This condition was making it very hard for me to walk. However, even the thought of succumbing to a power chair was unfathomable to me. This system is for rehabilitation, and it is for people with disorders of the central nervous system.

We put on a light-weight cuff worn below the knee, a gait foot sensor which is placed inside of the shoe and on my wrist, a wireless control unit. The units all communicate wirelessly to basically stimulate the muscles that cause the foot to lift. My therapist and I were truly amazed at how much I benefitted from it. My insurance did approve our request, and now I am able to walk more naturally using less energy and effort. Another good thing is that my chances of tripping up over a rug have decreased. My Bioness is my gift from God.

When I was young and healthy my role model was "That Girl," the young aspiring actress "Ann Marie," who lived in New York City. She was played by actress Marlo Thomas. Later, it was "The Bionic Woman," "Jamie Sommers," a PRO who almost dies as a result of an accident and is put together bionically. She suddenly has bionic skills, and the actress was Lindsay Wagner. Now, my hero is ME, and whenever I discover myself in the midst of some difficult, exhausting, very strenuous or unfavorable situation, I continuously repeat to myself, usually aloud... I can do all things through Christ who strengthens me. Philippians 4:13 NKJV

I drove a Buick compact luxury sedan. Although, I loved it, a car did not allow me to transport my scooter when fully assembled. I wasn't able to put it together all by myself. Therefore, I needed a Crossover or a small Sports Utility Vehicle (SUV). I did not want an exterior scooter ramp/lift. Instead, I preferred an interior lift. I chose to buy a Buick Crossover and had a Bruno interior hoist-style lift installed.

Me and my little bug "Pearl" (the name I gave to my Crossover), were well-equipped with my walker, rollator, my lift, scooter, a large amount of confidence and a very high dose of self-esteem. I felt like I was back in business. I was now well prepared to continue living the independent, worry-free life to which I was accustomed. Yes, I was definitely "The Survivor." Daddy gave me the perfect nickname. I could see how my lemons were beginning to turn into raspberry lemonade... my favorite, and it was so refreshing.

September was finally here. It had been a whole year since I saw it last. It was my most favorite month of the year. It was my birthday month, and for the second time in my life, I decided to give myself a celebration.

The first one was when I was in my mid-40s. A friend of mine who loved to cook and entertain had one of those upgraded, attractive and inviting new kitchens. Everyone would congregate in the area where she and her brother who had a culinary degree, prepared a fabulous and delicious meal. She had it remodeled for this reason. She loved having people over. We would gather around the island in the middle which separated it from her den. It was a large open space where we would even play cards sometimes.

I remember inviting almost everyone I knew. I got the idea the day before my birthday. I asked her to do the cooking, and I would buy all of the groceries. The party was so much fun. So many of my friends and associates came. Someone suggested dancing, so we moved the party to her living room. My friends were eating cake and dancing. We were having such a good time. I wanted to dance so badly. I had not tried since my diagnosis, except for when I was at home by myself listening to music. My balance wasn't very good, and sometimes my legs just refused to do what I wanted of them. Nevertheless, here was my chance to try, right? After all, I was around friends, and at least they weren't strangers. I let my guard down and decided to go for it. I was so glad I was brave because I had so much fun. I had the best time ever. However, I don't know what happened to my courage when they did the Soul Train line. I had faith, but I wasn't willing to test it that night!

This time I was turning 54. I chose to have the celebration at Ted's Montana Grill, a restaurant known for its Bison. I sent invites to 25 people. I reserved a dining area, so we would be tucked away from the other patrons. I remember sitting on my rollator and one of my nephews pushing me in because it was quite a walk for me from the parking lot to the front door. My friend who is a chef, made a delicious Key Lime cake for me with butter creme icing and pecans. It was a gift from his sister and my good friend... the one who gave my first party at her house. It was a wonderful evening, and we took lots of pictures. I actually propped myself up by holding on to a chair or leaning on the person who I was in the picture with. Almost everyone wanted to take a picture with me. I felt so very special.

There were friends from different walks of my life. Alecia (my friend from A&M, roommate at Westwind Apartments and now my real estate agent) and her husband were there. My friends even brought gifts. I came up with the idea to go around the tables and have each person tell their own personal story about how they were acquainted with me. Some made their account entertaining and original, and some of course, were merely nice and flattering. That idea was a hit and one of the highlights of my evening. It was all about me and my friends. It was a wonderful celebration!

I've learned that there are so many nice, caring people still left in the world today. There is always someone who seems to be in the right place and exactly at the right time, just when I need them. Unfortunately, there are also those who feel that because of my disability, it's inconvenient to involve me in their social activity. People can be impatient and lacking in understanding because they are unable to comprehend my challenges. Instead of judgment, if they felt empathy, they wouldn't be so hard on me and others with disabilities. With that being said... again, when I am faced with situations which challenge my abilities, I just repeat my favorite scripture... "I can do all things through Christ who strengthens me," and the Holy Spirit never fails to help me.

In the story about my life, I was turning Lemons into Raspberry Lemonade, and today whenever I am faced with adversity, I try to make the worst experiences the Best Ever!

"You Were Given This Life Because
You Are Strong Enough to Live It."
Unknown

CHAPTER 12
Daddy's Home

I only wished Daddy could remember. After all, he gave me this name, "The Survivor." My daddy was now suffering from dementia. Yes unfortunately, it was the exact same condition that afflicted his father, Grandpa Merritt. It was a like a spirit, harassing my family. I don't know if my sister did, but I never thought about it happening to my daddy, even though he was getting older. My mind just didn't go there regarding him. I began to visit them in Alabama much more often. Having the scooter was a big help because they lived in a senior assisted living building. The walk to their apartment was lengthy for me, even with the aid of my assistive devices. My nephew, KJ went with me a couple of times. I asked him because I didn't think it was very wise to travel that distance and be on the highway, alone. Besides, he was quite helpful. He put my scooter together for me whenever we would go.

There were times when I did go by myself. Daddy suffered a heart attack when he was in his 80s. Lula called and told us much later. He was still in the Intensive Care Unit (ICU). My mind began to ponder. I was probably over thinking it, but I needed to have been informed much sooner. This was my daddy, and although we didn't always see eye to eye on things, I loved him more than he probably realized and more than she could ever imagine. I called Ms. Baxter, his ex-friend in Huntsville. I was sure she would want to know. She often told me of how she still cared for my father.

I was able to get to the Huntsville Hospital late the next morning. I was in a hurry, for in my mind, too much time had already passed. I was mindful of the speed limits, being careful not to exceed them. Ms. Baxter gave me the address when I called her. I was grateful for her help, and I relied on my vehicle's navigation system to take me there. I was so thankful for this built-in feature. I did not have to read directions, for that would have required too much thought. No, all I had to do was concentrate on the other cars which shared the highway with me. A full tank of gasoline would more than get me there, and I would fill-up before coming back home.

When I pulled into the parking lot of the hospital, I could see that it was already almost full. The available spaces were much too far away from the front entrance. So, I pulled my car up to the facility's front doors. I saw that they offered valet parking, and an attendant was standing by to take me all of the way to my father's room in a wheelchair. It was an offer that was none other than a blessing. Since, I did not have to think about getting myself there, while we were in route, I took the opportunity to pray to my Lord and Savior, Jesus Christ. I thanked Him for saving my father's life and for bringing me to him. I gave thanks for His traveling mercy and for blessing me with His guardian angels, who by making the journey with me, ensured that I made it there safely. They were still with me... helping me, so I didn't have to use all of my energy, for I would need it when I saw him. Lula already told me to be strong and to control myself. The way I took it, she almost warned me not to cry. She was thinking of her husband, and although he could not see, she didn't want him to feel any negative energy. Of course, I totally understood.

When I entered the room and saw him lying there, he seemed to be facing the other way toward a window. He didn't realize I walked in, so I softly called his name. I had just transferred to my standard walker, leaving the wheelchair in the hallway. So, I went around to the other side of the hospital bed. I smiled because I could now see his face. I told him I was there, then he said my name, "Shirley"? I smiled again and answered. It was at that moment, when I felt a little better.

Her sister and brother-in-law arrived. A few minutes later her son came. I was so glad just to be there, for I was his family too. After we visited with Daddy for a while, Lula's brother-in-law who was a minister... prayed, and we all left the room together including my daddy. I assumed the nurses were dressing him for our visit. However, that was not the case. There would be no bracing myself

206

in order to hold back tears. Little did I know, he was being released. Praises to God and hallelujahs were in order, not tearful good-byes.

My step-brother suggested that I stay the first night over at their house with them. He explained how this arrangement would give our parents some time alone on his first night back home from the hospital. I was hesitant at first because I didn't want to leave my father so soon after arriving, but then I quickly realized he was right. The next day would be soon enough for me to be near Daddy. After all, he was in the best of hands.

They had moved into a much larger independent, single family apartment. I parked close to their unit and simply used my rollator to walk in. Cynthia, KJ and Brian called that evening. I was sitting on the sofa across from him while they talked. I could see in his facial expression and hear in his voice; how happy he was to hear from them. What I also noticed and did not quite understand was that he never mentioned to them that I was even there. I tried not to dwell on it because honestly, what mattered to me was that... I was there. God wanted me to be there, and I came.

My father gave me the greatest surprise. I had just swallowed my meds when I heard Daddy and his rollator come into the living room where Lula made a bed for me on the sofa. He made his way over to a dinette chair that was pulled away from the table. He must have been able to see its outline because he knew that it was there. I sat up and reached for the lamp, to turn it on. Daddy asked me to help him sit down. I guess since I wasn't very visible, he forgot that I too was disabled. Even so, it made me feel good when he asked for my assistance. It felt quite similar to a blind leading the blind scenario.

Daddy began our heart-to-heart discussion. We talked for hours, covering many things but mostly about our little family... back in the day. I told him about the love of my life, my baby girl, Penny. She is my shih-tzu doggie. I fell in love when I first laid eyes on her and held that little puppy in the Pet store at the mall. She is the child I never had, and she loves me unconditionally. One employee told me she was a miniature. Another one said she was simply the runt (weaker or smallest) of the litter. Regardless, I paid 1100 dollars for her, and I named her Penny. Never buy a dog from the mall. FYI, the prices are escalated, especially on a purebred with a pedigree. With that being said, I wouldn't have traded her for the world, and if I bought a less costly shih-tzu from a breeder instead, well... she wouldn't have been Penny, would she?

After sharing my feelings for my baby girl with Daddy, he said in an uncompassionate way, "I could never feel that way about a dog." Be that as it may, I was there to be kind and loving, so I just kept what I wanted to say all to myself. Besides, I knew that he only felt that way because he's never had to be alone. When you live by yourself, especially if you are disabled, it can get lonely, and you will gladly welcome a furry friend who wants to share their life with you. The sad thing is that unfortunately, our pets don't live forever. I suppose we want them to live as long as we do. However, they have very short lives in comparison to ours.

My baby girl means the world to me, and Penny was actually abducted once. I had her in the yard so she could run and play for a while. She was just a little puppy, but I thought she would be okay for an hour or less. My nephews were there, and I asked them to check on her. When I came home she was gone. She had been taken from underneath the fence. She was mine for only a couple of months, but I had already developed a bond and didn't want to be without her. My legs would not support me if I tried to find her myself, so I got an idea, and I asked my nephews to help me. Brian went to the park with me because a kid on my street gave me a lead that she might be there. She said some boys were attempting to sell her, but I knew she had a microchip inside. I pulled up next to some boys and asked if they had ever seen her. The one who seemed like the leader said, "No we haven't."

We printed a photo of her. I made 8 by 10-inch copies. KJ and I posted them on telephone poles in the neighborhood next to the park. In a couple of days, a boy called and told me he found her. I met him at his address, gave him a 100-dollar reward and never let her out of my sight (figuratively speaking), again. By the way, the boy who called was the same boy I approached in the park. While she was missing, I prayed to God, holding her blanket and a plaque that read... EXPECT A MIRACLE, close to my heart. I purchased it at a women's conference at my aunt Bettye's church in Dallas. I told God, I needed her. So, for that reason, I've always called her my miracle dog. God brought her back because He gave her to me.

How much that little girl means to me, truly amazes me. I cannot imagine my life without her. I'm thankful that I don't have to think about it now, but I suppose the day will come when I'll have to figure it out somehow. I'm going to cherish this time I have with her. It's hard to be sad when she's around... a bad mood is almost never. It's so true, what they say about man's best friend. Their unconditional love is the best love ever.

At the time when I brought my baby girl home, I already had a little boy. He was a beautiful black feline. I've never really been superstitious. I've never felt the need to walk around one in order to keep it from crossing my path. He came into my life when he was just a little fur ball. He was beautiful to me. There were many times when he put a smile on my face and kept me from being lonely, so he was more than welcome to take up residence in my home. He was almost 10 years old when he died. Cats and dogs don't usually get along, and that was the case with my pets, at first. However, once he got used to her being around, I guess he decided that she wasn't that bad after all. She was never afraid of him, even though he was twice her size. She would jump on his back, chase him around and even wrestle with him. She finally won him over, and they became the best of friends. Often, I found them napping side by side with their arms intertwined together. Once, I found them with their arms around each other. Thank God for cellphones with picture-phone. I made sure to "Capture the moment."

Actually, Midnight was my second cat. I had an orange and white Tabby, 25 years ago. Bam-Bam was his name. I gave him away when he was three years old. I was young, and I guess I hadn't quite yet developed the strong belief that I have now which is that you should never adopt a pet if you don't intend to keep it for the rest of its life.

We had been talking for hours when my meds decided to kick in. I heard Daddy say, "Are you falling asleep"? I realized that I must have nodded off while I was talking in mid-sentence or something because I just knew, he couldn't see me. I told him about taking the meds and how I was very surprised, they didn't remind me that I ingested them hours ago. It was meant for us to have that quality time together. It was the best conversation he and I ever had in my entire life. I wouldn't have wanted to be anywhere else in the whole wide world than in his living room, sleeping on their sofa-bed which was not so comfortable... that night. Funny, it was now 7:00 in the morning. I always felt that Daddy and I shared a special bond. However, I'm sure, Cynthia could have felt the same way. We were both Daddy's girls, and he never made a difference between us.

Later, in September of 2015, Lula called to tell me that Daddy's condition was progressing, and he was now bed-ridden. A nurse from hospice was coming by several times a week. Hospice provides care for the sick and terminally ill, and it is run by a religious organization. This part of our lives happened during the five-year estrangement between my sister and me. We were still alienated from each other. So, we did not ride together. I reached out to my oldest nephew, but this time, which was the worst possible time, he declined my request to accompany me.

I was out having lunch with two sweet young ladies who I met one day at my MS clinic. We called ourselves, "The Sisterhood." We picked a restaurant and met once a quarter. We even brought each other gifts. Gloria had no visible disability. She seemed strong and healthy, just like my sister. In fact, she always helped both me and our mutual friend. Shawn always used a cane because she also had some mobility challenges. Although hers weren't as acute or bad as mine, they were visible. I mentioned my father and the date that I was driving to Huntsville to visit him. They both said they wanted to go with me. I said, "Really"? Hearing the girls say that touched my heart. I really didn't want to go alone, but of course I prayed about it, and I would have because nothing was going to keep me from being with my daddy.

Coincidently, I was contacted by a dear childhood friend. It was perfect timing because I was going to be in Alabama soon. We made plans to meet for dinner because we hadn't seen each other since high school. It would be nice catching up with each other's lives. She and her sisters were the only girls that Daddy let us have sleepovers with when we were kids. I was looking forward to seeing them again in Huntsville, but visiting Daddy was my priority.

We left Atlanta and took I-20 W toward Birmingham, then we took I-65 N to Huntsville. I drove all of the way to Daddy and Lula's. I was using my navigation system, so we didn't have to be concerned about the directions. When we took the exit to Huntsville, it was approximately 24 miles from I-565 to US-72, which turned into University Boulevard. We made a couple of more turns, then we arrived at their apartment complex.

I called Lula from the vehicle to let her know we were there, and she came outside to greet us. I introduced her to Gloria and Shawn. They were so happy to meet her. They hugged her as if they were seeing her again, not like it was their very first time. It was a confirmation to my spirit that I brought the right ones with me. We followed her to their unit. She was tiny and much shorter than I. I never noticed that about her before. She said she'd be back in a minute because she wanted to check on my father. When she returned from their bedroom she said he was sleeping right now, and she didn't want to disturb him, but she would wake him up soon. So, we sat down and visited with her for a while. We chatted about pleasant topics. We wanted to take Lula's mind away from things for a few moments.

This precious, sweet woman loved my father unconditionally, as he also loved her. I have never seen a more perfect example of soulmates than my dad and Lula. He was her Boaz, and she was his Ruth. Lula said, "Let me see if he's awake now," and she went to

211

check on him again. Then she told me to come on back, but before I went in she quietly said to me, "Brace yourself and be strong."

Daddy was frail. Lula forewarned me that he was weak and had lost a lot of weight, but because he was Daddy, I only saw a very strong man, and even the MIGHTY can lose a battle. I said, "Daddy" and he answered, "Shirley"? It meant so much that he knew who I was. As soon as he knew I was near, he puckered his lips just like he always did, and I kissed him. You can only imagine how I felt. He knew it was his "First born," even though he didn't say it this time. Then he asked me if I was able to pull a chair up close. I told him that I could. When he asked me if I was comfortable, I smiled and said, "yes." At that moment, I was sure that although he didn't look like himself anymore, he was still very much my daddy.

I spent the next hour or two back there in the room with Daddy. We reminisced about the past, and he remembered. I asked him some questions about his life... like when he was a mailman, and with a little probing, he answered. I played guessing games with him when he couldn't think of the answers... or at least, when they didn't come quickly. Instead of him playing the "Girl from Ipanema" for me on his saxophone... this time, I sang it for him, and he smiled.

Lula came into the room to see what was going on because she and the girls heard the sounds of our laughter all the way in the living room. Later, she shared with me that she hadn't heard him laugh like that in years. If she only knew how much joy that brought to me, and she said he heard the tune on the radio that day.

Daddy talked about Heaven and how he could hardly wait to get there. To spend forever with his Lord and Savior, Jesus Christ (El Shaddai), was what he had been living for... He was looking forward to seeing his friends and loved ones who had gone on before him. His eyes opened wide and became bright when he spoke about Him and even just the thought of it all.

Later, I asked Lula if my friends could come back and meet my father. She said, "yes", and she was just thinking about that very same thing. I remember Gloria helping Lula to sit him up. Lula gave him his medicine, and then we all chatted together. Before we left for our dinner, Daddy asked if we could all sing a nice spiritual song together. So, I thought of one of my favorite hymns sung by Bishop Larry Trotter, and I led the song...

Sweet Holy Spirit.
Bishop Larry Trotter

and just before we all finished our melody, Daddy's voice imitated a saxophone, the way that he always used to do, which gave it such a special ending!

I went to Huntsville again in January of 2016. The dementia was worse. In the past, ever since he lost his sight, he always told me the color that I was wearing. I guess, he could see it with his peripheral vision because he was always right. This time, he finally got it wrong. Lula sometimes described his episodes, and they were now more frequent. She told me about how he would tell her about a wonderful woman that he knew who took care of him. He would go on and on about her. He would even describe her home, and she knew he was talking about her.

On a Sunday in March of the year 2016, Daddy transitioned into his Heavenly body and went to meet his Maker. He was 90 years old. Daddy was cremated, and a Veteran's Military Burial Ceremony was held in Birmingham, Alabama at his grave site.

Nervously, I was near the end of the procession line, but God was faithful for He intervened. A man yelled, "Let her by," so I could drive up through the middle of the cars which were parked on each side of the street leading to the pavilion. It was sort of like when Moses parted the Red sea. I saw my nephews and asked them to carry me. Otherwise, I wouldn't make it in time. It was hard to move through grass with a walker, and they were trying to figure out how to pick me up... when all of a sudden, a stocky young man dressed in denim overalls walked up and said, "I'll do it." He carried me as if I was a baby, and the way a groom carries a bride. He put me down in a seat that was empty because it was designated for me. It was between my sister Cynthia and Lula.

I made it just in time, for the officer was playing the bugle. "Taps" is the song that is performed at military funerals. They folded the military funeral flag and presented it to Lula. It was there that my sister and I spoke for the first time in five years. We rekindled our relationship after Daddy had passed. I do believe he whispered something in God's ear, asking Him to help us find our way back into each other's lives. It's been said that from death comes new life.

Later, I looked for the man who carried me in. I wanted to thank him because if not for him, I would have missed the ceremony. When I found and met him, he told me his name was Demetrius, and he was the first child and student to graduate from their founded El Shaddai Inner City Ministry Christian Academy. Needless to say, I felt very privileged and honored to meet him. My sister and her family-including her in-laws and me and the three friends who came with me, all had dinner together before leaving Birmingham.

A few months later in the summer, his beloved wife and the now-grown-up children of their El Shaddai Ministry, carried on and held their annual reunion. However, this year it was special. It began with a cherished Memorial service where my father's great legacy was honored, and some of the board members were there. It was also a celebration for Lula's 80th birthday. I miss my daddy and will forever love him. I will see you again one day Daddy... in eternity, and you were the Best Father Ever. Whatever his Favorite Flavor... Daddy's Lemons were now his Lemonade!

A couple of years ago my sister Cynthia was on a job assignment in Pasadena, California. She called Daddy to get the exact address of our old home on Loma Alta Drive because Altadena was only 15 minutes away. She and her colleague went there after work one day. They decided to ring the doorbell. By her own account, she cried as they approached the doors. She recognized them because they were the same double doors with gold windows. The residents had not changed them in 50 years. The moss and ivy landscaping which Daddy planted all of those years ago was still there and exactly the same.

When the owners answered the door, she told them her name and that she lived there 50 years ago. They told her, James Merritt sold the house to them. They invited her in. She tells me, the long hallway we remembered, was actually very short. She said the house was tiny, yet we thought of it as big. I guess we were just so small back then. When she asked why they had not changed the doors and replaced the moss with grass, they told her they loved it just the way it was. They also said the big and tall tree in the yard was no taller than the little girl she was... when we moved. The wife told her that my mother's spirit influences her decorating skills. They also said it was their dream house.

Cynthia said when she told Daddy about her heartwarming visit to our old home in Altadena, his eyes filled with tears and he said, "It was our dream house also."

"Daddy I know you are up in Heaven playing melodic tunes with Gabrielle... for the angels and His Majesty."

Shirley A. Merritt

CHAPTER 13
Giving Thanks in the Midst of Trouble

Due to the progression of my illness, I have developed different challenges. I thought about the people who God placed in my life. He situated these remarkable individuals throughout my existence. Each one of them was used as an example for me. He strategically positioned them, as if they were part of a road map of my journey and a glimpse of what was yet to come.

First, was my dear friend with the underdeveloped leg because I gradually lost the use of my right leg. Then there was Lindsay-with the one arm because over time, I've lost and am still losing function and the full use of my right arm, hand and fingers. In the end, my brother Peter had muscle spasticity and a weakened body, making it difficult for him to even get out of bed. These are symptoms and results in which I am all too familiar with sometimes.

Then there was Alton. Although, he was still beautiful in the end, he did have severe nerve damage. He even lost his ability to speak and swallow. I can relate to each one of these a little, and for a while, slurring was a major symptom. It was a large part of why I had to stop working. Alton lost the function and agility of his fingers. These symptoms definitely affect my ability to type, write and use my fingers proficiently. When Daddy was losing the function of his hands and fingers and his ability to walk, we often compared our disabilities. We were surprised at how much we had in common and how these different diseases shared many of the same symptoms. Bernard experienced weakness and paralysis as I do.

Today, most of the people I call friends, have either no visible disability, much like my sister, or it's very minimal. They might have fatigue and balance issues or pain in their legs (neuropathy) which they experience when walking distances. They might use a cane occasionally, for some additional support. Most of my friends own canes, and some of them own rollators. Like myself, one even owns a scooter. However, their devices are more for precaution reasons.

They are rarely required to use them. I consider them to be blessed. However, I also feel that I am surely blessed because I am able to live independently. I try to be self-sufficient. Of course, there are some varied tasks which I require some help with, and when I do, God sends someone just as He promised. Since I only have the full use of just one of my arms and hands, certain chores such as changing the linens on my bed are very hard to do. Vacuuming the steps has become too difficult, not to mention dangerous. Changing light bulbs is really next to impossible because of balance and right upper extremity and dexterity problems. However, it is as if God said, "No worries, I've got you." He has blessed me with a cleaning service and a gifted new washer and dryer via the Multiple Sclerosis Foundation (MSF). Amazingly enough, driving my vehicle has been unaffected.

I am grateful for The Multiple Sclerosis Society, for they have provided me with a wellness and gym membership. This privilege allows me to be able to exercise at a Brain and Spinal cord injury rehabilitation center. This organization also, awarded a "Service day" for my home a couple of years ago. The interior of my house was painted, and a few major repairs were addressed. This gift was truly a blessing, and the contest is annual.

There is a very helpful organization called The Multiple Sclerosis Association of America (MSAA). This organization will provide wheelchairs, walkers and canes, leg lifters, and many other assistive devices for those in need of them. They also assist with MRI co pays.

I am thankful for these organizations because they exist to help make life easier for those of us who have the various challenges that MS presents.

I am also very thankful for the friendships God has given me, for without good friends, life wouldn't be much fun. We have different friends because they each serve different purposes. You've heard the saying, "You can't choose your family," and well, we all know that is true. However, we definitely choose our friends. Sometimes, we make mistakes with our choices. Even so, the good thing is that we can always remove ourselves and carefully choose new ones whenever we feel the need or desire to do so.

I have some favorite scriptures and quotes that remind me to be thankful even in unfavorable circumstances...

1 Thessalonians 5:16-18 KJV in everything give thanks for this is the will of God in Christ Jesus concerning you. (Daddy taught us this one).

Romans 12:12 ESV Rejoice in hope, be patient in tribulation, be constant in prayer.

Be thankful for the difficult times; during those times, you grow.
Be thankful for your limitations because they give you
opportunities for improvement.
Be thankful for each new challenge because it will build your
strength and character.
Be thankful for your mistakes; they will teach you valuable
lessons.
Troy Amdahl

This past Easter Sunday, my sister, nephews and I went to dinner at the popular restaurant, Red Lobster. I was using my walker when my nephew came up with a better idea that would make things easier for me. He carried me into the restaurant and through the dining room to our table. I'll be honest, I wanted to close my eyes, but instead, I just smiled at everyone as they made room for us to come through and was very thankful for him and his compassion. At the end of our meal, our waitress said, "I have a surprise for you." She told us that our party's entire meal was paid for by some kind anonymous person. Needless to say, we were all so overjoyed and extremely thankful for the kind, heartfelt blessing we received on Resurrection Day!

After writing this memoir, if I have been able to help change the mindset of even a few individuals, whether you are living with a life-changing illness or just trying to remain positive and survive in everyday life, I will feel that I have achieved my goal, and it was well worth my while. My aim is to inspire and motivate others. So, if you feel as though you've been given lemons, turn them into something better. Make it something great, then add your favorite flavor!

One of my challenges is the loss of function and the ability to fully use my dominant right arm, hand and fingers. Writing this memoir has probably been my greatest challenge and achievement. I created the story in six months, typing it with two fingers on my left hand and my thumbs. All of the praises go to my Heavenly Father. I am most thankful for the wonderful, close relationship I now have with my Lord and Savior, Jesus Christ. It is a cherished blessing which has blossomed and strengthened through my MS journey.

In spite of the lemons which I have been handed during my life, I've managed to turn them into my favorite... Raspberry Lemonade! I've learned to make The Worst Experiences, The Best Ever!

"The Lord is my strength and shield. I trust Him with all my heart. He helps me, and my heart is filled with joy. I burst out in songs of Thanksgiving. Psalm 28:7 (NLT)"

WEBSITE REFERENCES

http://www.history.com/this-day-in-history/the-first-american-in-space

https://en.wikipedia.org/wiki/John_Glenn

https://en.wikipedia.org/wiki/Altadena,_California

https://en.wikipedia.org/wiki/Huntsville,_Alabama

https://www.vonbrauncenter.com/vbc-history/

https://www.microsoft.com/en-us//store/music/album/prince/for-you/8d6kgx7m2wr3

http://www.aamu.edu/Pages/default.aspx

https://en.wikipedia.org/wiki/Parisian_(department_store)

https://www.riverchasegalleria.com

https://en.wikipedia.org/wiki/Carpal_tunnel_syndrome

http://www.webmd.com/multiple-sclerosis/guide/what-is-multiple-sclerosis#1

https://www.bioness.com/Home.php

https://en.wikipedia.org/wiki/Fresno,_California

https://en.wikipedia.org/wiki/San_Antonio_River_Walk

https://en.wikipedia.org/wiki/Layoff

www.nationalmssociety.org

www.msfocus.org

www.mymsaa.org

https://www.sharecare.com/health/multiple-sclerosis-causes-risk-factors/is-multiple-sclerosis-hereditary

ABOUT THE AUTHOR

Shirley A. Merritt earned her bachelor's degree in clothing and merchandising at Alabama A&M University in Normal, Alabama. She is retired from a 24-year career in the Telecommunications Industry. Shirley is very active in the Multiple Sclerosis Community as an advocate. She has collected over $2300.00 in donations toward research for the MS Society as a participant in the MS Walk Atlanta 2015-2017. Shirley recently placed #57 in the top 100 for Atlanta in 2017. As an author and writer, Shirley enjoys reading, traveling, cooking, listening to various genres of music, spending time with her pets and of course, writing. Shirley currently resides in Atlanta, Georgia.

Life is always going to present new experiences and challenges. We must learn to accept, adjust, perfect and conquer them. When we don't, we will be held back and even left behind. When we do, we will be successful, happy and fulfilled.

Shirley A. Merritt